WRITING THE HISTORY PAPER

WRITING THE HISTORY PAPER

**How to Select,
Collect, Interpret,
Organize, and
Write Your
Term Paper**

By

David Sanderlin
English Instructor
Miramar College

Barron's Education Series, Inc. Woodbury, N.Y.

All inquiries should be addressed to:
Barron's Educational Series, Inc.
113 Crossways Park Drive
Woodbury, New York   11797

Library of Congress Catalog Card No. 74–694

International Standard Book No. 0–8120–0506–6

Library of Congress Cataloging in Publication Data

Sanderlin, David.

   Writing the History Paper:
The Student's Research Guide.

   SUMMARY: Investigates the definition of history,
how it is written, and how it should be read.
   Bibliography: p.
   1. Historical research.   [1. Historical research]
I. Title.
D16.S255   907′.2   74–694

ISBN 0–8120–0506–6

my parents

Contents

Preface

This is a guide to historical and interdisciplinary research for undergraduate students of both history and related disciplines. The book can be used as an introduction to history by college as well as high school students: what history is (Chapter One), how it is written or created by the historian (Chapters Two through Seven), and how to read it (Appendix II). Since reading history is simply identifying and analyzing what an historian has written, an appendix on reading history is a logical conclusion for any instruction about historical research and is an important part of this guide.

I have written this guide because I believe that the college undergraduate can do original research; that is, he can, through reading or research, choose and pursue on his own what he would like to know. Unfortunately, college history students are seldom asked to develop, upon the basis of their interests and experiences, their own visions of the past. They are asked not to be historians, but to understand and analyze the theories of historians, or even just to repeat them. However, people are likely to commit themselves less to the theories of others and more to those truths which they perceive from their own experiences; hence few undergraduates today seem to care deeply about what they learn. Of course students can seldom be professional historians, but they can be amateurs; they can do, at their level, what historians do. I wish to help students to develop their own ideas so that they may be amateur historians, so that they may be individuals, so that they may be people who believe in and care about what they know.

This guide should be particularly appropriate for those instructors who offer students an active role in their own education by granting them some freedom to pursue their interests. I do not, however, value "relevance" over "scholarship": scholarship (that is, thinking with precision) is relevant, and relevance (that is, thinking with conviction about what matters) is scholarship at its finest. Frequently scholarship and relevance are falsely separated; I seek both, not only for historians, but also for students of history.

Lengthy research manuals often overwhelm undergraduates who cannot assimilate, much less apply, four hundred pages of information on research and writing. Students need not know fifteen rules for preparing footnotes or three methods of note-taking. They need know only the fundamentals: how to conduct research, how to write, how to think. I have written only what is necessary to guide students in the development of their ideas about subjects that matter to them.

I have supplemented traditional research procedures with a new method of collecting information in libraries with open stacks. This new method (Chapter Three, pp. 27–33) and short but detailed outlines of the Dewey Decimal and Library of Congress classification systems (Appendices III and IV) should serve the undergraduate researcher well. Instructors can facilitate for their students the use of the method of systematic browsing by preparing detailed outlines of the sections of their own school library which yield material on the subject matter relating to their specific courses. For a medieval history course, for example, a three-page outline of medieval sections of a library might include the following entries: medieval and Renaissance philosophy (call numbers B 650–B 785), history of Christianity (BR 50–67, BR 165–280, BR 741–754, BR 1700), Bible (BS 425 ff.), medieval civilization (CB 245, 351–359), medieval history (D 111–202), history of England (DA 110, DA 150–300), medieval London (D 677–680), France (DC 62–106), Germany (DD 125–151) and so on (e.g., Italy, folklore, cartography, recreation, political theory, law, education, music, art, literature, science, medicine, warfare).

Although I alone am responsible for this book, I do thank

both my parents, for their critical reading of the rough draft, and my wife, for typing the manuscript and for the continuing inspiration she provides.

D.G.S.

Introduction for the student

Summarized below are seven steps (corresponding to the seven chapters in this guide) in the preparation of an historical research paper. You should, of course, ignore any directives in this guide which, given the nature of your subject or the wishes of your instructor, cannot or should not be applied. Your chief aim should be to develop your idea about a subject of interest to you—not to follow blindly every suggestion in this guide. If, for example, you cannot use primary sources, then use what is available to you.

STEP ONE: *identify history.*

You should first understand why you conduct historical research. Reflect upon the nature of history: what it is and why and how you study it. Read Chapter One of this guide.

STEPS TWO AND THREE: *select a subject and collect information.*

Read Chapters Two and Three. In selecting your subject, it may be helpful to browse in different sections of the library to see the kinds of information available. Also, you might begin with several possible subjects, and choose that topic for which you locate the most interesting information.

STEPS FOUR AND FIVE: *interpret and organize your information.*

So that you will know what to look for and what to record when you collect information on your subject, read Chapters Four and Five, on interpreting and organizing material, at an early stage in your research.

Organize your facts, prepare a rough outline of your paper, research further, reorganize, refine your outline: in short, develop your understanding of your subject, formulate your conclusion.

STEP SIX: *write your paper.*

Read Chapter Six. Write rapidly a very rough draft and more carefully a second one. Revise your draft by deleting unnecessary material, clarifying vague ideas, identifying terms, and so on. Write a final draft and prepare footnotes and bibliography. Type the paper, if possible (double-spaced, with corrections in ink if acceptable and legible). Proofread the paper and turn it in.

STEP SEVEN: *reflect upon the present.*

Read Chapter Seven. You might compare your subject to something similar in your contemporary world, or you might consider what your study reveals about yourself, your society, or mankind. Consider how your knowledge of writing history might be applied in reading historical works (see Appendix II).

1

The Historian Astride His Hobbyhorse

Bill Tilden, a great tennis player of the past, is said to have remarked that it would require at least five years of daily practice to become a tennis player; similarly, professional historians might insist that one at least have a Ph.D. before being considered an historian. However, since there are not only professionals and experts, but also amateurs and beginners, I shall be less exclusive: anyone who plays tennis for several months is a tennis player of sorts, and anyone who studies history at college is an amateur historian. You, as a reader of this guide and a student of history, are an historian because you do what the historian does: you study the past. You should, therefore, understand the historian's craft.

History is an academic discipline in which people living in a present time seek to understand the significant communication of people in past societies.

History is the study of past societies; in particular, it is the study of the people in those societies. The historian strives to understand people, not merely to recount events. And it is not easy to understand people; let us take the case, for example, of an historian in the future who might seek to understand why American college students rioted in May, 1970. It would not be sufficient for such an historian to conclude simply that the students rioted as a consequence of President Nixon's extension of U.S. military involvement from Vietnam into Cambodia; this explanation would reveal neither why the students protested this particular extension of this particular war, nor why they protested by rioting rather than, for example, by addressing letters to their president. People's actions do not follow necessarily from preceding events (the riots need not necessarily have been caused by Nixon's extension of the war); rather, people choose to act, and to act in a particular manner. Events, then, only suggest why people select a particular course of action. Because of the influence of the military draft, approaching final exams, poverty in America, spring sunshine, acquaintance with violence on television, and other factors, American college students—when they learned of the extension of the war—chose (whether consciously or subconsciously) to riot. People, either as individuals or as groups, make events. It is people whom the historian must understand.

The historian must understand the role in history not only of the people in the past, but also of the people in the present. History, which is really a story of the past, exists only in the mind of the storyteller, who is the historian in the present; thus the historian must understand how his present mental vision of the past represents the past as it actually was.

The historian develops his vision of the past by investigating historical records, records that reveal what people in the past chose to reveal or to communicate about their world. Thus history is an attempt by people in a present time to understand the communication of people in their past. Just as children have difficulty in understanding their parents, separated from them by a single generation gap, so will the historian have difficulty in understanding people in the past, separated from him by immense generation and cultural gaps. People, past and present, have difficulty understanding and communicating with one another. If we reflect upon the nature of communication, we might learn to understand better not only our ancestors across the centuries, but also our neighbors across the street.

We communicate through language and actions, but often we misunderstand and are misunderstood. For example, suppose a high school teacher, wearing an unconventional red and purple tie with pink stripes, explained to his students that he wore the tie to please his wife, who gave it to him for Christmas. The students would interpret the teacher's action and statement differently: a show-off might conclude that the teacher wore the tie to attract attention rather than to please his wife; an individualist might think the teacher enjoyed wearing the tie in scorn of convention; a student who had received similar unconventional apparel as gifts from relatives might accept the teacher's statement at face value. These students would have been prepared by their experiences to assess the teacher's actions differently; thus our ability to understand others is limited by our experiences which, together with heredity, have determined our character, our individuality, our unique way of evaluating people and viewing the world.

I shall call this individuality of perception and interpretation a hobbyhorse. Everyone views the world from astride his hobby-horse, that is, his experiences which have prepared him to see the world from a particular perspective. A hobbyhorse is a child's toy, a stick with a horse's head at the top. A child on his hobbyhorse is in an imaginary world: his father is an Indian chief, his mother a squaw, the refrigerator a wagon train. And each of us dwells in an imaginary world created by his own experiences. The teacher is perhaps not a show-off, not an individualist, not a dedicated husband, but we can never know precisely and with certainty what he is, for we do not see reality face-to-face. We are all children on hobbyhorses.

The image of a hobbyhorse has been used before to illustrate a problem of communication. The eighteenth-century English author Laurence Sterne used it in his novel *Tristram Shandy*. For Sterne, the hobbyhorse represents an individual's ruling passion: "When a man gives himself up to the government of a ruling passion,—or, in other words, when his HOBBY-HORSE grows head-strong,—farewell cool reason and fair discretion!" The hobbyhorse of one character in the novel, Uncle Toby, is military history, as a consequence of his war experiences. When another character speaks to Toby of a train of ideas, Toby recalls a train of artillery and responds with a discussion of weapons and warfare. Thus we learn from this exaggerated example that because of our different experiences we all assign different meanings to the words by which we seek to communicate.

Like Uncle Toby, we all ride hobbyhorses, for we are all particularly aware of certain aspects of reality. Young children are especially aware of candy, boys like baseball and other sports, teenagers thrill in the discovery of the opposite sex. Perhaps the most common hobbyhorses are health, sex, and a desire for security and success.

Our hobbyhorses affect our vision; we see what we have been prepared by our experiences to see. Individuals will notice different things while walking to a store: a boy might see bugs on the sidewalk; a street cleaner, litter on the street; and a pilot, airplanes in the sky. We do not see every detail within the range of our visions, for we are not cameras recording photographic images, but people receiving mental images which represent the world not as it is, but as our minds have prepared us to see it.

Thus we see different worlds from astride our hobbyhorses. Just as the students saw the same teacher as show-off, as individualist, and as dedicated husband, so historians develop different interpretations of the same events. These interpretations often more accurately reflect the experiences and characters of the historians than they capture the essence of the past. The student of history must, therefore, be careful lest his vision of the past be a vision only of himself. History, we see, is not a dull record of facts and dates; it is a fascinating attempt by people on the hobbyhorses of one generation and culture to understand the communication of people on the different hobbyhorses of earlier generations and cultures.

PRIMARY SOURCES

The communication of people in the past is available to the historian in primary sources of information. A primary source is a source of information dating from the period of history being studied. Coins minted by a Roman emperor, roads constructed by Roman builders, letters written by Roman citizens—these are primary sources for the study of Roman history. A secondary source of information dates later than the period of history being studied. Edward Gibbon's *History of the Decline and Fall of the Roman Empire*, written in the eighteenth century, is a book written about an earlier historical period and is a secondary source for the study of Roman history. Textbooks are secondary sources. I shall use in this guide the definition of a primary source given above. However, a primary source can also be defined as an eyewitness account of an event. A reporter's description of an accident he witnessed would be a primary source; a secondary source would be the account of a reporter who had been told about, but who had not witnessed, the accident.

The historian depends upon primary sources: without records surviving from the past, he would have no evidence for his conclusions. Primary sources are most readily available as books in libraries. Dante wrote the *Divine Comedy* in the fourteenth century; this primary source has been translated from Italian into English and published as a book. Many primary sources are available in any college library.

UNCERTAINTY OF HISTORICAL KNOWLEDGE

Primary sources do not reveal the past in its entirety. Records for the majority of men's thoughts and actions were not kept. Those which were recorded have too often been lost or neglected, buried in desert sands or library archives; others have been destroyed by disasters such as fire and flood and war. Because the historian can never be sure that he has all the facts pertinent to his inquiry, he can never be certain that his conclusions are valid.

Also, the historian cannot be certain of his conclusions because primary sources were produced by people on hobby-horses and are, consequently, distorted reflections of the past. Thus, because primary sources are only partial or distorted visions of the past, and because the historian himself rides a hobbyhorse and has a distorted vision of those primary sources, historians cannot discover precisely and with certainty either what happened in the past, or what people in the past believe happened. History, then, may be a fascinating discipline in which people on the strange hobbyhorses of one generation seek to understand people on the equally strange hobbyhorses of earlier generations. But why study history if we cannot discover what happened in the past? How can the communication of people in the past be significant if it cannot even be understood? What can be the purpose of studying history?

We study history to understand better the people in past societies and thereby to better understand ourselves.

Contemporary historians, struck by difficulties of communication such as those outlined above, have been pessimistic about the value of studying history. However, we should be not discouraged but encouraged by our intense awareness of the problems of communication, for we cannot solve a problem unless we are aware of it. If we recognize the difficulties of communication, we may speak and listen with greater care; we may learn better how to understand one another.

UNDERSTANDING PEOPLE IN THE PAST

Of course we can never understand one another completely and with certainty because, as has been noted, each of us is isolated by his unique experiences. I cannot understand what you mean by the word pain because I have not had your experience of pain. But we need not choose between understanding one another completely and not at all, for there are varying degrees of understanding between these extremes. Although I have not had your experience of pain, I have perhaps had a similar experience, which might enable me to understand in some degree what you mean by the term pain. We can, then, understand one another to some extent. Although it is true that we cannot understand one another completely (that is the price we pay for our unique individual experiences), it is equally true that we can understand one another to a degree because of our similar human experiences.

But we need not despair that we cannot understand one another completely and with certainty, for all human knowledge is limited. The laws of science, for example, have been formulated only upon the basis of the limited experience of the human race up to the present moment; our universe might be regulated by cyclical laws, unknown to us, which change every 4,000 million years, and tomorrow a new cycle might begin that would make rocks fall up, not down. I cannot know with certainty that rocks fall down, that I am awake and not dreaming, that my friend is sincere when he yells at me to watch out for the truck. But I would be foolish not to dodge a rock released from above or to look out for an onrushing truck, simply because I was not sure that the rock would fall down or that my friend was sincere when he yelled that a truck was coming. We do profit both from our scientific knowledge and from striving to communicate.

Although our knowledge is limited, it serves us well.

UNDERSTANDING ONESELF

The historian, then, can understand to some extent and learn from people in the past. He hopes to learn from them truths which he had not recognized from his own experience. He imaginatively mounts their hobbyhorses that he may see reality not from his own limited perspective, but from the wider perspective of mankind. From the saddles on the hobbyhorses of people in the past, the historian can see for the first time his own hobbyhorse, his limited vision of reality, himself. The historian strives to understand people in the past that he might better understand himself. Thus does he follow the advice of the sage: "Know thyself."

The historian may conduct any investigation which might help him understand himself. One who constantly tripped over doorsteps, for example, might study ancient Romans who had the same habit. Such an investigation could lead to a significant understanding not only of the historian's own habit of tripping over doorsteps, but also of Roman society—for example, Roman methods of construction, Roman medical practices (care for people who stumbled and broke their legs), or Roman attitudes toward suffering (upon breaking a leg). The intelligent investigation of any subject can lead to a better understanding of the past, for whether an historian identifies his topic as Romans tripping over doorsteps, the utensils and recipes of Roman housewives, or Roman civilization, it is people in society whom he strives to understand—Romans in the past and himself in the present.

We study history by historical thinking.

Since history is a discipline in which people in a present time seek to understand people from the past and thereby themselves, let us consider how this goal can best be achieved.

Whether historians read books, attend lectures, write papers, or visit museums, they study the past by thinking about it. Thus it is necessary to understand how they can think about the past most effectively and what manner of thinking is most proper for the historian.

HISTORICAL THINKING DEFINED

The thinking of historians during the Middle Ages resembled that of the theologian; in the eighteenth and early nineteenth centuries it was similar to that of the philosopher; and for the remainder of the nineteenth century it was very like that of the scientist. Historical thinking in the twentieth century, however, is likened neither to theology, philosophy, nor science, because human events are no longer seen as acts of God, manifestations of reason, or scientific facts. For example, history is not science, because the historian cannot discover why the Roman Empire fell with the same degree of certainty as the scientist can discover why apples fall.

Because the historian's vision of the past is distorted by his experiences, some twentieth-century scholars have suggested that historical thinking resembles the self-expression of the artist more closely than the objectivity of the scientist. Others have compared history to psychology and sociology, two disciplines, which have like history the goal of understanding people. But the historian cannot, like the artist, disregard the facts entirely; he must try to understand what actually happened in the past. And the historian does not, like the psychologist and sociologist, formulate principles about man and his activities, but strives only to understand individual persons and groups.

Contemporary historians, then, have been unable to liken history to any other discipline, and have reached little agreement about the nature of history and historical thinking. There has been, in fact, a cry of despair: what is history?

This inability to identify history as another discipline need not lead us to despair. Knowing that history is not theology, not philosophy, not science, not art, not psychology, not sociology, not mathematics, not dancing, we are prepared, perhaps for the first time, to discover what history is. Our inability to liken history to another discipline might indicate that, having witnessed past ages dominated by an emphasis on theology or philosophy or science, we are now on the threshold of an age of history. In any event, let us identify once and for all the manner of thinking proper for the historian, that is, historical thinking.

Historians in all eras have utilized common sense; they use common language, they stick to the facts. But the historian today has learned that historical facts are not facts, but distorted representations of reality. And common sense fails the historian who strives to understand people, for people do not act upon principles of common sense any more than upon scientific, philosophical, or theological principles. Common sense tells the historian that people should not build houses near active volcanoes, but people do build houses near active volcanoes.

What manner of thinking is proper for the historian, who has traditionally used common sense, but who strives to understand people on strange hobbyhorses? The answer, of course, is common sense about people on other hobbyhorses, or, in short, hobbyhorse sense. Historians can best understand people in the past and thereby themselves if they apply the three principles of historical thinking identified below and elaborated upon in subsequent chapters of this guide.

The historian learns from history most significantly if he develops his own vision of the past.

General knowledge can be distinguished from individual knowledge. That the Roman Empire fell in the West in 476 A.D. is a fact in man's store of general knowledge. That fact becomes part of one's individual knowledge if he relates it significantly to his own experience—by reflecting, for example, that the declining Roman civilization from the third to the fifth centuries is similar to his American civilization in the 1970's. It is not necessary, however, that individual knowledge be related to contemporary events. The historian cannot only relate the past to the present, but can also relive it in the present, that is, for example, make the fall of the Roman Empire his own contemporary event by "experiencing" it intellectually in his present. In either case, significant learning is not the acquisition of facts of general knowledge which mean little to an individual, but rather the development of individual knowledge, of one's own vision or understanding of the world which he experiences.

Each historian must identify for himself what is significant, for no one else sees the world as he sees it from astride his hobbyhorse. The historian will be less likely to acquire individual knowledge if he passively absorbs those historical theories which others have considered significant without selecting those topics relevant to him and with them developing his own story of the past. It is not enough for the student of history to read, give opinions about, or critically analyze books assigned by his instructors, for such exercises do not allow him the freedom to pursue his interests, to strive to understand himself and his world. Furthermore, the student who is asked only to repeat, give opinions about, or critically analyze the thinking of others, never learns to think for himself, to develop an idea of his own. It is one thing to criticize the play of a quarterback or the thinking of a scholar; it is quite another to play the game or develop an idea oneself.

The historian learns by discovering truths revealed by the experiences of people in the past which he had not recognized from his own experience.

We learn when we discover truths which we had not previously recognized from our experiences, but what we have not recognized we often reject as untrue. Perhaps an adaptation of a medieval theory of a double truth will prevent us from rejecting too quickly what does not seem true upon the basis of our experiences. Just as some medieval thinkers distinguished those truths revealed by God from those deduced by reason and proposed that one accept both truths, though they might appear contradictory, so we can distinguish those truths revealed by one's own experiences from those revealed by the experiences of others and accept both truths. If we recognize that people in the past, as well as in the present, have discerned truths not revealed to us by our experiences, we will be more likely to listen to, and perhaps learn from, their communication. For all of us discern some truth. A criminal who slays a man to obtain money for food recognizes the truth that it is good to eat, though he ignores or fails to see the truth that people should not be murdered. Most individuals hold larger portions of truth: Republicans and Democrats, bachelors and married men, pacifists and fighters— something can be said for both sides.

We will never understand, much less learn from others, if we condemn them for not knowing what we know, rather than respect them for knowing what we do not know. Communication and understanding, even love, are possible only with a humble awareness of the limitation of our own vision of the world and a respect for the visions of others. Only, in fact, by denying ourselves and imagining what it would be like to see the world from astride another's hobbyhorse can we finally communicate with and understand one another.

The historian must identify the distortions in his own vision and in those of people in the past.

The historian cannot accept whatever people in the past reveal; he must not only empathize, but also criticize. The experiences of people in the past revealed some truths about reality, but obscured others. The historian must consider all factors that might have distorted the visions of people in the past: for example, age, religion, nationality, historical period, occupation, sex, and political affiliation. Further, he must consider how these same factors (*his* hobbyhorse) may have influenced his own understanding of their communication.

The preceding principles of historical thinking can be applied when reading books, attending lectures, or writing papers; we shall be concerned in this guide primarily with the latter. Writing a paper is the most effective way you can learn to develop an idea yourself. Furthermore, after completing a paper, you will understand from experience how historians have developed the theories you read in history books. In short, writing a paper can help you understand better what it means to think, and this understanding is the only solid foundation for an education.

HISTORY TODAY

History itself, furthermore, is perhaps the ideal discipline for the common man. It does not require a specialized training. The historian is not limited in his investigations to literature, political theory, or science, but can roam freely through all man's past activities: the housewife, the plumber, the scientist, each can pursue his or her own interests as amateur historians. And history can perhaps answer questions currently troubling many of us. We are concerned about the fragmentation of knowledge, and history, touching upon all disciplines, can provide us with a coherent vision of the totality of human activities; we are troubled also by the inability of individuals within a community to communicate with and understand one another, and history, which trains one to understand people in past societies, can show us how to understand and care for one another.

History, in short, is about understanding people, ourselves as well as others. And, as indicated by our concern with such things as sensitivity groups, sociology, civil rights, communes, witchcraft, and relevance in education, we are today concerned with people, both as individuals and as members of society. Perhaps we have entered an Age of History.

2
The Historian
As Selector

The historical researcher is satisfied neither with the theories of the past which other historians have developed nor with the vision of reality which he has inherited from his society. He believes that he can develop a more accurate and significant vision of reality, past and present. The researcher cares about the way he sees reality; he loves it enough to put his own mind to it and to touch it, to taste it, to experience it intellectually for himself. The researcher clears his own path to the truth, he carries his own lantern—quite simply, he searches. This chapter is about selecting a subject for your research, identifying a personal approach to the truth, riding your hobbyhorse into the past.

IDENTIFY YOUR INTERESTS,
EXPERIENCES, AND GOALS

The historian studies the past that he might better understand himself; in selecting a subject, then, identify first your ultimate subject, yourself. What do you know and wish to know about yourself, about the way you see reality? Identify your significant experiences, interests, and goals. A student in a medieval history course, for example, listed the following aims and interests: mysticism, mythology, Hopi Indians, riding horses, and teaching high school. These items are the ingredients of a single subject:

comparisons between Hopi Indian, mythological, and medieval mystical attitudes toward animals and nature. This is an excellent topic for the following six reasons:

1) By combining subjects, the student can pursue several interests in his research for one paper. An interest in warfare, in agriculture, and in family life, to provide another example, could be pursued in research on the single subject: the effect Civil War battles had upon the agricultural production and family life of Southern farmers.

2) By combining the Hopi Indians and medieval mysticism, the student can relate a past course (American history) to a present one (medieval history). Thus he can develop a body of knowledge organized around his interests and experiences, rather than one delivered to him in separate courses or chunks of knowledge related only chronologically.

3) This student will be able to use his knowledge of medieval society when teaching American history in high school, because he has related medieval mysticism to the Hopi Indians. Education can be in part a preparation for employment: prospective doctors or nurses might investigate the history of medicine, businessmen the role in history of business and trade, farmers the social impact of improvements in agricultural methods, and housewives past methods of raising children. Such investigations might make students more aware of the historical significance of their vocations, suggest ideas for the conduct of their businesses, or simply help them choose rewarding occupations. (After writing a paper on the medieval physician, a girl remarked that she would like to become a doctor.)

4) The student's subject, incorporating several of his interests, is unique. Many scholars have studied medieval mysticism, but few in conjunction with mythology, horses, and Hopi Indians. With scholarly works on his specific subject unavailable, he will almost have to develop his own ideas, rather than simply to

repeat those of others. He will see the past (medieval mysticism) from the unique perspective atop his hobbyhorse (Hopi Indians, horses, mythology).

5) Relating his personal experience of riding horses to mysticism might help the student empathize with medieval mystics and the Hopis in his investigation of their attitudes toward animals and nature.

6) The student's selection of several subjects effects the limitation of his topic by establishing the perspective from which it will be viewed (as noted above, mysticism viewed from the perspective of one interested in mythology, horses, and Hopi Indians). It is usually insufficient to limit a subject by establishing chronological, geographic, or other arbitrary boundaries; a study of English games in 1850, for example, might involve consideration not only of many games, such as football, tennis, and chess, but also of a bewildering variety of questions about games, such as who played them, when, where, and why. A subject is most effectively limited by identifying a particular aspect of it, such as mysticism limited to the mystic's attitude toward nature, and a particular question about it, such as how mystical attitudes toward nature compared with Indian religious beliefs.

LOCATE PAST EVENTS RELATED
TO YOUR INTERESTS

In selecting your subject, then, consider your experiences, interests, future occupation, and goals, and draw from these a single topic which combines at least two different subjects. Having considered your ultimate subject, yourself, identify the immediate object of your inquiry in the past. An interest in horses can be pursued through a study of Hopi or Franciscan attitudes toward animals, and one in the Vietnam war through an investigation of World War I, the Civil War, or the Crusades.

Whatever interests you have identified in the present can be pursued in the past, because history is about people, and human concerns have not changed greatly over the centuries.

IMAGINE HOW YOU MIGHT PURSUE YOUR SUBJECT .

Having tentatively identified your subject, imagine where you might look for information and what you might find. Suppose you have selected the subject "games." Perhaps educators discussed the role of games in education; maybe preachers delivered sermons about their influence on children's moral standards; possibly changes in recreational interests affected the economy of a country. If, for example, you have not imagined beforehand that you could use the ideas of preachers, you will not look for a collection of Christian sermons. If you are prepared to "see" in your research only the word identifying your topic, e.g., "games," you will find only books on games. Historical research requires imagination; you imagine the facts, then discover them.

And you must stick to the facts you discover. Since you cannot write what you imagine or hope to find, do not insist upon answering a particular question, for an answer may not be revealed in available records. Be prepared to change your subject slightly. Investigate attitudes of Roman aristocrats, rather than peasants, if you discover that, since the peasants were illiterate, their opinions were not recorded.

SAMPLE SUBJECTS

The following list of research topics selected in upper division history courses indicates the variety of subjects which might be pursued:

1) Witchcraft/cooking/medical use of herbs, equals (=) the single subject, comparison between witch potions, food recipes, and medical prescriptions.

2) Child-raising/education/leisure = the role of recreation in the education of children.

3) Town life/marketplace/trade and prices = prices in markets.

4) Black Death (plague)/mysticism = impact of the Black Death upon religious values.

5) Transportation/gold rush/California history = transportation during the California gold rush.

6) American women/recreation/twentieth-century journalism = coverage of recreational activities for women in American newspapers since World War II.

7) William the Conqueror/peasants/daily life = comparison between the working conditions of English peasants before and after the Norman conquest by William the Conqueror.

Although the variety of subjects which might be investigated has been emphasized in this chapter, do not hesitate to study typical historical topics, such as very *limited* aspects of Greek democracy, the fall of the Roman Empire, feudalism, the French Revolution, the Civil War, and British imperialism. The following are general areas from which more limited topics could be selected: political history (wars, political intrigues), economic history (trade, business), social history (role of women and children, superstition, daily life, class struggles), and the history of religion and other disciplines, such as music, math, science, and art. The historian, of course, will investigate the historical, rather than technical, aspects of related disciplines (e.g., Wordsworth's attitude toward nature in its historical context, rather than his poetic diction).

Note the following list of historical events and topics from which subjects limited to a narrow thesis might be selected:

Babylonian animal sculpture
Babylonian hymns to Gods
Hammurabi's law code
Egyptian astrology
Egyptian conquests under Thutmose III
Hebrews—monotheism

Athenian democracy
Peloponnesian Wars—naval battles
Death of Socrates
Aristotle, political theory
Hippocrates, medical study of the anatomy
Roman army discipline
Sanitation in Rome
Gracchi—agrarian reform
Roman attitudes toward nature
Christian attitudes toward suffering
St. Augustine—concept of history
Hunger in medieval chronicles
Machiavelli, *The Prince*
Italian banking
Patriotism in Shakespeare
Calvin—predestination
Thirty Years' War in Germany
Bartolome de Las Casas—plans for a New World utopia
Charles I of England (1625–49)—taxation
Education of Peter the Great of Russia (1689–1725)
Early world maps (15th–17th centuries)
Baroque painting and the Catholic Reformation
Voltaire—Enlightenment idea of the natural goodness of man
Maryland Toleration Act (1649)
Salem witch trials (1692)
Treatment of Indians in colonial America
Communication in colonial America
American Revolution—economic causes
Declaration of Independence (natural law)
French Revolution—storming of the Bastille
Monroe Doctrine (1823)
Hair styles in 19th-century America
Morality in the American West
Napoleon—military tactics
Factory system (Industrial Revolution)
Child labor
Jeffersonian democracy
American attitudes toward European culture
Slavery and Christian sermons
Romanticism (Thoreau—civil disobedience)

Death in Romantic literature
Darwin—evolution and creation
Pope Leo XIII (1878–1903)—private property
Cooking in Victorian England
World Wars I and II
Social impact of the automobile
F. D. Roosevelt—New Deal
Korean War
American circuses
Whaling
Beverages
Tramps and social outcasts
Children's names
Clocks and time-awareness
Prison reform
Fire fighting
Diet
Log cabins and comfort
Indian medicine
Riots and strikes
Marriage customs
Shopping centers
Smuggling
Bathing
Vaudeville
Campaign slogans
Morality in American advertising

ALL HISTORICAL SUBJECTS
INVOLVE PEOPLE

Some subjects lend themselves more readily than others to the approach to history outlined in Chapter One. Students investigating past attitudes towards women, for example, may more easily discover distortions in their attitudes and those of people in the past than will students of agricultural technology. However the latter subject as well as the former requires an understanding of people. Why was a certain improvement in agricultural technology made by a particular person or society at a specific time and place? Why did people choose to develop new equipment for one kind of crop in one section of a country, and not for another in another section? The researcher might consider the influences of education, geography, and the economy, for example, in striving to understand why certain people developed particular agricultural methods; that is, he might consider the educational, geographic, and economic experiences of people on hobbyhorses.

Similarly, the historian of music concludes not simply that certain songs were sung, but rather that these people chose to sing about these particular subjects, in this specific manner, rather than about other topics in other styles. Why did people choose this method of bringing up children, this style of art, this manner of waging war? One cannot complain that little can be done with his subject, that he can only state the obvious facts, for the historian not only states the facts, but also attempts to understand what they mean.

3

The Historian As Collector

Having selected a subject, you are prepared to collect information, which is available primarily in libraries. The ability to locate information in a library is a prerequisite for students who actively pursue their own interests rather than passively absorb from lectures and assigned texts those ideas considered most significant by their instructors. This ability to use a library can be drawn upon throughout one's life, whether in locating stimulating reading material for one's children, conducting research in preparation for a new job, or merely entertaining oneself with a good book.

Three methods of collecting information in libraries are summarized below: that of the scholar, that of the average undergraduate, and a new method which I have devised and shall call "systematic browsing."

Scholarly research

The scholar locates information by using reference works, such as encyclopedias, atlases, historical dictionaries, guides, and bibliographies. A bibliography is a list of books or other sources of information on a particular subject. A bibliography may be a list at the end of an article or book, or even an entire book in itself. *The Bibliography of Costume* by Hilaire and Meyer

Hiler, for example, is a list of titles of books and other sources of information on costume. The scholar, after locating in this bibliography the titles of works pertaining to his research, could find these works in the card catalogues of his own and other libraries (the card catalogues of large libraries, such as the British Museum, the Library of Congress, and the library at the University of California at Berkeley, are frequently available in other libraries). Using bibliographies and card catalogues, then, the scholar can locate books from around the world and obtain them through inter-library loan.

The undergraduate need not consult bibliographies and other reference books to locate all the material pertinent to his subject, for he usually desires only that information readily available in his college library. Every undergraduate, however, should be familiar with at least two types of reference books: encyclopedias and guides. Encyclopedias provide the researcher with bibliographies (printed at the conclusion of each entry) and short identifications of subjects. Most students could profit from a more habitual use of encyclopedias, not so much for the articles on their research topics, as for those on related subjects which they need not investigate in depth.

Guides are books written by experts to direct others in their fields of expertise. There are guides, for example, to buying houses, to travel in Europe, and to coin collecting. Every history student should be familiar with the standard guide to history: The American Historical Association's *Guide to Historical Literature* (New York, 1961). This guide is an annotated list of the titles of the most important reference books, primary and secondary sources, periodicals, and other sources of information on all historical subjects. In studying the medieval Papacy, for example, one might locate in this guide not only the authorities on that subject (e.g., Horace Mann, *The Lives of the Popes in the Middle Ages, 590–1304*), but also the most useful reference works and collections of sources for research in medieval history (e.g., the periodical, *Speculum*, and the source collection, *English Historical Documents*). *The Guide to Historical Literature* (N.Y., 1961) can be supplemented with bibliographies published more recently in encyclopedias, books, and periodicals.

Every college student, whether in history or in any other discipline, should be acquainted with a second guide, Constance Winchell's *Guide to Reference Books*, 8th ed. (Chicago, 1967). This guide is an annotated list of the major reference works in all branches of learning; it is a guide to the entire library. One seeking reliable information on, for example, the French Revolution, Victorian physicians, or international laws, could locate in Winchell the AHA's *Guide to Historical Literature* (which lists authoritative books on the French Revolution), Garrison's *Introduction to the History of Medicine* (which identifies authorities on the history of medicine in the Victorian era), and the United Nations' *Treaty series: Treaties and International Agreements Registered or Filed and Recorded with the Secretariat of the United Nations* (which provides the texts of international treaties).

In using Winchell's guide, ignore the titles of books in foreign languages and of books of limited scope; Winchell's short descriptions of the works listed should help you find the ones most useful to you. Conducting research in English literature, for example, you might locate the *Cambridge Bibliography of English Literature*. Winchell describes it as "the most extensive and comprehensive bibliography in its field." F. W. Bateson's *Guide to English Literature*, published too recently to be included in Winchell, could be located in a second guide to reference material, by Walford, which can be used to supplement Winchell (see Appendix I, A). For a list of important reference works in history and other disciplines, see Appendix I (pp. 73–75). Note especially the *Harvard Guide to American History* (listed in section A of the appendix).

Undergraduate procedure for collecting information

The undergraduate typically uses the card catalogue of his library to locate books on his subject, and notes the sources used by the authors of these books. The cards in the card catalogue are filed alphabetically by the author, title, and subject matter of the book (Cash, W. J., *Mind of the South*, under "C" for the author, "M" for the title, and "S" for the subject matter, the South).

The following is a typical library card:

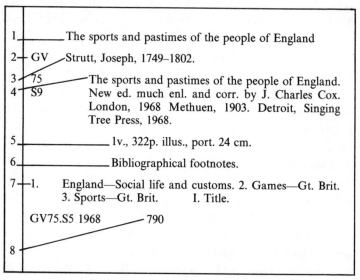

Note the following identification of the items on the card: 1) subject matter of the book (the title also in this case) 2) call number 3) author's name 4) title of the book, followed by the name of the publisher and the date and place of publication 5) identification of the book—one volume, 322 pages, with illustrations, portraits, and a height of 24 centimeters 6) bibliographical information (references to other sources of information on the same subject) 7) other subjects in the card catalogue under which the book is entered 8) Dewey Decimal Classification number.

Subjects are identified in card catalogues in many ways. Information on sports, for example, might be found under "Amusements," "Recreation," "Games," "Football," "Physical Education," "Universities—athletics," and "England—social life." Related subjects, such as health (physical fitness), will also yield material. The researcher must be imaginative in checking subject entries of the card catalogue. The subheadings of each subject classification should also be checked carefully; a book on cooking in fourteenth-century Paris, for example, might be filed under "cooking—French" rather than "cooking—history of."

Systematic browsing

Through the use of the card catalogue undergraduates have usually gathered the research of scholars on their subjects, rather than conducting original investigations. For example, those writing on the Black Death in fourteenth-century Europe have relied upon books on the Black Death, which represent the research of scholars on that subject. Students use less obvious sources primarily when led to them by scholarly references; here again they follow the research of others. It is not surprising, then, that their papers are often rehashes of the theories they collect.

If undergraduates collect facts rather than theories, however, and if they conduct their own research, they will be more likely to develop their own ideas. There is information on most subjects in many sections of a library. For example, there is material on the Black Death not only in books on the history of medicine (library call number R); the history of Christianity (BR); the Papacy and monasticism (BX); the histories of

England (DA), France (DC), Italy (DG), and other countries; the history of education (LA, LF); English literature (PR); and the history of science (Q)—for the Black Death had an impact upon the Catholic Church, the countries of Europe, educational institutions, and so on. The card catalogue does not reveal the location of this information on the Black Death; there may be one hundred library cards representing books on the history of medieval education, but there is no indication on these cards that the books contain information on the Black Death. Thus students, relying upon the card catalogue, seldom discover the abundance of material available in libraries.

I propose a new method of collecting information in libraries with open stacks. By this method the student may go directly to the books on the shelves; he does not have to rely upon the limited account of the library available in the card catalogue. Thus he can acquaint himself not only with the card catalogue but also with the library behind it. By walking directly to the shelves and browsing systematically among the books immediately available, he can locate a great deal of useful new information, so that his paper will be unique. There are four steps to this method of collecting information, which I shall call systematic browsing.

1. Identify the library sections most likely to yield information on your subject.

Books are arranged in most libraries by one of two classification systems, the Library of Congress and the Dewey Decimal; outlines of these systems are provided in Appendices III and IV (pp. 95–125). By skimming the Library of Congress classification (or the Dewey Decimal, if used in your library), you can identify the sections of the library most likely to yield information on your subject. The following are examples of topics and the library sections most likely to contain relevant information:

a) *World War II, role of navies:* D 731-838, DA, DC, DD, DG, DS, E 740-   , GC perhaps, HE 381-971, JX, V 750-980 (books about the countries involved in the war, international law, and naval history, for example).

b) *Witchcraft:* BF 1001-1999, BL 300-325, BR 140-1500, CT 3200-3830, DA, DC (and other countries), GR, K, Q, and other sections (witches might appear in church records, histories of countries, mythology and folklore, law, occult sciences, and so on).

c) *Woman and equality in American history since World War I:* Biography of women (CT 3200-3830), Twentieth-century America (E 740ff.), folklore (GR 440-950), customs—love, marriage (GT 2400-5090), marriage (HQ 503-1064), feminism (HQ 1101-2030), political theory—minorities (JC 311-323), laws of states, e.g. Alabama (KFA 0-599), education of women and special classes (LC 1390-5153), etc.

For topics within political or economic history, all countries (D-F), economic history (H), political science (J), and law (K) are normally important library sections. For topics within social history (for example, the role of women, cooking, superstitions, and recreation), all countries (D-F), folklore (GR), manners and customs (GT), recreation (GV), social history (HN), art (N), and literature (P) are important sections of the library. Certain library sections assume greater importance during particular historical periods; for example, archeology for ancient history and the history of Christianity for the Middle Ages. American historians profit by investigating European developments relative to their subjects, just as medievalists profit by studying Greek and Roman sources.

Thus there is likely to be a good deal of information on any subject in many sections of a library. One cannot always think of the appropriate topics to consult in the card catalogue (e.g., to check laws when writing on witchcraft), but one can skim the outlines provided in Appendices III and IV and discover many areas of the library which might yield information on a particular subject.

2. **Locate the relevant areas within each library section identified in step one.**

Sometimes any book in a given section of the library might yield information on a particular topic, as any book in the folklore section, GR, might provide material on evil spirits. Other times, however, useful books might be located only in certain areas of the section: for example, there may be hundreds or thousands of books on the history of England (DA), but if you are investigating the Black Death you would need only those books on England in the fourteenth century. The second step in systematic browsing, then, is to locate those areas within a library section which are most likely to yield information on your subject. Books in history sections are arranged chronologically, and books on countries both chronologically and geographically. The following diagram illustrates the arrangement of books on Great Britain (DA):

LIBRARY SHELVES: GREAT BRITAIN (DA)

(The books are arranged on the shelves in order from left to right, *a* through *c*, as the arrows indicate.)

a General histories of England (miscellaneous)	→			
b Limited studies of English history, arranged chronologically	Eng. 5th cent.	Eng. 8th cent.	Eng. 14th cent.	Eng. 20th cent. →
c Limited studies of England, arranged by geographical location	Southwest England	London	Wales (next country) →	

If you seek information on the Black Death, you can look through the shelves until you reach the books on England in the fourteenth century, London in the Middle Ages, and France and other countries at the time of the Black Death.

Although works on the histories of countries and other disciplines are arranged chronologically (e.g., history of philosophy—B, law—K, medicine—R), the arrangement of all the books within a given discipline is normally topical (e.g., medicine is divided into pathology, surgery, and so on). The outlines of the library in Appendices III and IV should provide you with sufficient identification of the library sections to locate the areas most useful in your research.

3. Scan the shelves and select those books appearing most useful.

You cannot examine every book in a library section containing 50 to 500 books; hence you must identify, by noting the titles on the backs of the books, those most likely to yield information on your subject. You should examine three types of books: primary sources, books of limited scope, and works on subjects related to yours.

Primary sources should always be examined. They are identified by titles such as *Letters of* . . . , *Sermons of* . . . , *Chronicle of* . . . , *Diary of.* . . . Books "edited," "translated," or "compiled" by an author indicate that he did not write the book, but collected or translated what others (frequently people in the past) have written, and thus such books are often primary sources. Collections of sources with titles such as *English Historical Documents* and *Sources of Indian Tradition* are especially valuable because they provide in a single work source material on many subjects.

Even though a primary source may not bear directly upon

your subject, it does reveal the thinking of the people you are trying to understand. For example, an American colonist in a letter to a friend might have defined superstition. This definition would help anyone who is investigating colonial medicine to understand how colonists might have distinguished superstitious medical remedies from scientific ones.

Researchers often forget that a society's underlying philo- sophical (library call number—B-BJ), religious (BL-BX), social (H), and political (J) assumptions help determine how people choose to raise children, what they sing, how they treat minorities, what laws they pass, what leaders they support. Primary sources revealing these assumptions should not be neglected.

Books of limited scope, such as *A Baronial Household in the Thirteenth Century*, are usually more helpful than more compre- hensive works, such as *England in the Thirteenth Century*; the former will yield little-known facts about a single English household, whereas the latter will probably provide only well- known information on English history in the thirteenth century. Ignore the multitude of books of broad scope.

All books on your subject or related ones should of course be examined. If you are investigating cats in ancient Egypt, for example, check books on cats, animals, domestic life, social history, and other related subjects. For political subjects, examine books on contemporary leaders and events that might be related to the men or activities you are investigating.

4.   **Check the indexes and/or tables of contents of the books selected in step three.**

In the final step of systematic browsing, check the tables of contents or indexes of the books located in step three. Books on literature or art seldom have lengthy indexes, although lists of illustrations are often provided in the latter. Subjects might be entered in an index, just as in a card catalogue, in many ways; information on punishments in colonial New England, for example, might be found in an index under punishment, torture, stocks, pillory, trials, witches, criminal punishment, and a variety of other possible entries.

To summarize, in the method of systematic browsing, you skim the outline of the Library of Congress (or Dewey Decimal) classification system and secure the call numbers of those library sections most likely to yield information on your subject. Then go to the shelves in these sections and skim the titles of the books. When you locate a book that appears useful, examine its table of contents or index. If the work provides relevant information, keep it; if not, reshelve it. By this method you will find many books that are likely to yield information on your subject and that are immediately available (not checked out, or located only in other libraries). Also, you conduct your own research; hence you are able to develop your own story of the past with information which has not been presented by other historians in just this way.

Although you will probably develop your own individual method of recording information, note how I have summarized material on the following sample note card (a 5″ x 8″ index card, not the smaller 3″ x 5″ or 4″ x 6″ size):

BX2260M31965

McNeil, John, and Helena Gamer, *Medieval Handbooks of Penance*, N.Y.: Octagon Books, Inc., 1965. Pp. 153, 246, 330 [references to witchcraft].
Source material on witchcraft in medieval handbooks of penance (penalties ascribed for sins).

p. 331—Burchard, German bishop, 11th century, assigns penances for *beliefs* that witches could, by invoking devils, arouse tempests, change men's minds, steal, ride on beasts on special

---

nights, etc. One-year penance for such beliefs compared to 10-day penances for seeking oracles or prophecies (p. 331, no. 67).

Another penitential, Irish, 6th century, shows that . . . (continued on next card)	Witchcraft/ Church attitude/ 6th–10th centuries

1) Write a complete and correct bibliographical identification of the book: author, title, publisher, date and place of publication. Then you will be able to prepare your footnotes and bibliography from your notes, thus saving a great deal of time.

2)Indicate the pages containing the material you summarize. This may be important for verification of your facts if questioned, or you may need more details, quotations, or footnote references.

3) Identify on each card the nature of its information: e.g., witchcraft/laws/10th century; witchcraft/folklore; or Church-/definition of heresy; thus you will be able to locate all your material on laws, folklore, and Church attitudes when you are ready to draw your conclusions about them.

4) Record important information in detail (e.g., authors, chronology, and facts, such as that Burchard, a German bishop, eleventh century, assigned penances for *belief* in, not simply practice of, witchcraft). You cannot conclude from your notes that attitudes toward witchcraft changed from one year to the next if you do not know the dates of your sources. It should help you to record intelligently the information you collect if you read the following chapter, concerning your interpretation of such material, before you begin extensive research.

4

The Historian As Interpreter

The information you collect must be interpreted. Since your attempt to understand the statements and actions of people in the past is similar to your endeavor to understand people in the present, the following guidelines for interpretation can be used whether you are examining an ancient chronicle or discussing politics with your neighbor.

1. Identify the perspectives of people in the past.

You will be better prepared to understand a person's appeal for the development of smog control devices for automobiles if you know whether he is a forest ranger, politician, or potential smog-control manufacturer. Identify the perspectives of people in the past not only by gathering biographical information but also by observing what they say or do. Consider not merely what an individual might be expected to be, given factors such as his age, nationality, religion, and educational training, but what he is by what he chooses to say and how he chooses to act. Also when reading an historical source, note what people said or did, and then imagine what they could have said or done.

2.   Consider the audience for whom an action is intended.

Does the politician propose smog-control devices before a gathering of conservationists or of automobile manufacturers? Is he revealing his own hobbyhorse or appealing to those of his audience?

Consider also the nature of this action: is the politician writing a personal letter or delivering a campaign speech? Private letters are more likely to reveal personal feelings than are campaign slogans; different kinds of sources (such as letters, laws, chronicles, art, and literature) yield different kinds of information. In determining the nature of the information a particular source yields, remember one simple rule: a campaign speech is a campaign speech, a private letter is a private letter, a law is a law, and so on. Let us take the case of a law. A law is a law, that is, a prohibition of certain actions, but *not* a record of them. Police records reveal alleged crimes, but laws reveal only that people passed laws against crime. More laws against crime, then, means more laws against crime, not necessarily an increasing crime rate. Prohibition laws prove not that drinking increased during the Prohibition era, but that certain people chose to prohibit drinking. Laws reflect changing perspectives as well as changing conditions.

Consider another example: legislation in California around 1970 curtailing excessive expenditures in the state's system of higher education. Now unnecessary expenditures by institutions are regular occurrences. In California in the late 1960's, however, taxpayers saw such normal conditions as a new problem; expenditures previously ignored were noticed with alarm and curtailed by legislation. This legislation was a consequence not so much of excessive spending as of other factors, such as the diminished willingness or ability of tax-payers, pinched by inflation and rising property taxes, to continue the same level of support for education. As a consequence, in part, of an economic recession, higher education was viewed from a new perspective. Therefore the legislation reveals not only changing conditions, but also changing attitudes.

Just as a law is a law, so is a sermon a sermon, that is, a religious statement. A Christian preacher may urge his congregation to be good Christians—for example, to beware the wiles of wicked women. He need not present in a sermon his private opinions, e.g., that women may be kind, generous, devout, and intelligent. One cannot conclude from sermons that Christian preachers did not respect women, for in a sermon there is moralizing, just as in criminal records there is evidence of crime, and in political speeches, there are campaign slogans.

3.   Identify the date of an action.

A proposal for smog-control devices does not mean in 1945 what it does in 1975; in 1945 it implies that the speaker is farsighted. Does an individual ride a hobbyhorse ahead of, or behind, the hobbyhorse of his era? And what accounts for that hobbyhorse? Why, for example, do the people of one generation choose to develop smog-control devices, or to support Prohibition laws? The historian strives to understand why an action occurred at a particular time.

4.   Identify the facts revealed by an action.

Identify the facts revealed by an action. For example, a German Catholic bishop in the eleventh century made the following statement about witchcraft in a handbook of penance (a book listing the penances, or penalties, prescribed for sins):

> Hast thou believed or participated in this infidelity, that there is any woman who through certain spells and incantations can turn about the minds of men, either from hatred to love or from love to

hatred, or by her bewitchments can snatch away men's goods? If thou hast believed or participated in such acts, thou shalt do penance for one year in [*sic*] the appointed fast days.

Of the many facts revealed in the passage above, let us note four: a) Bishop Burchard considered it a sin to believe that witches could enchant people b) some Christians believed in witches c) there were beliefs that witches "turned men's minds" and stole goods d) those who believed that witches could enchant people in the manner specifically described were required to do penance on appointed fast days [fasting on bread and water].

5. Your interpretation should be your identification of an actor and his action.

Your initial interpretation of an action is your identification (rules 1–4) of the actor and his action. For example: the politician, speaking to his wife on April 1, 1945, suggested that smog-control devices be developed for automobiles; or, Burchard, a German bishop in the eleventh century, wrote in a handbook of penance that Catholics who believed that witches could enchant people were to do penance for one year.

You cannot conclude what you have not identified, for example, that the Catholic Church considered belief in witchcraft a sin, because you have identified the position of only one bishop, who represents, but does not equal, the Church (other bishops might have made different statements about witchcraft). The historian can generalize only when he accumulates enough similar individual cases.

In the above interpretations we have, as good historians, stated the facts. But we selected only those facts which we considered significant; we noted, for example, that the speaker was a politician, but not that he was a Buddhist. Thus, even when historians state nothing but facts, they can, by selecting different facts, develop conflicting interpretations of the same events.

The historian not only states facts but also draws inferences or implications from them. Does the fact that the politician spoke to his wife imply that he was sincere in his support for smog-control devices? Always offer at least one reason which confirms your inferences; for example, the inference that the politician was sincere because he was speaking to his wife is confirmed by the fact that his wife did not discuss her husband's opinions publicly, and thus could not be used politically to leak information. The inference has been confirmed by the selection of another fact, that the politician's wife does not gossip. Thus interpretation is the identification and selection of facts.

6.   Compare actions.

We understand things by comparison; *talkative* means one thing to Trappist monks vowed to silence, and another to gossiping women. To understand the statement about witchcraft by the German bishop, Burchard, we compare it with other statements. Consider the following record of a fourteenth-century English trial for individuals accused of witchcraft:

> [In 1324] . . . when . . . Richard, Bishop of Ossory, visited his diocese, he found by solemn inquisition, whereat were five knights and a great multitude of other nobles, that there had been in the city of Kilkenny, and still are, very many witches, practising divers sorceries which savoured of heresy. . . . [Of these] heretics and sorcerers . . . some were publicly burned in due course of law . . . others banished from the city and diocese.

Let us note only one of the facts revealed in this passage: an English bishop and nobles found certain persons guilty of witchcraft and identified them as heretics. Thus, whereas a German bishop in the eleventh century considered belief in the existence of witches a sin, an English bishop in the fourteenth century not only believed that witches existed, but also found them guilty of heresy. Additional passages with similar evidence support the conclusion that the Christian attitude toward witchcraft changed during the High Middle Ages (1050–1300). The Church began to see witchcraft as an actual communication with real Christian devils, rather than a superstitious belief in the possibility of communing with pagan spirits which did not exist. Witchcraft became a Christian heresy, rather than a pagan superstition. By comparison, then, our passages about witchcraft are better understood.

7.   Mount the hobbyhorses of the people in the past.

You may correctly conclude that the English bishop believed that witches should be burned or banished, but a valid interpretation is not to be equated with understanding. You can understand people only by mounting their hobbyhorses; you must "be" the bishop. Imagine what it would be like to believe in angels and devils. Is this world not an eerie place, which could be peopled with spirits? And if there were evil spirits, would it not be despicable to invoke them for sinister purposes? Mount the hobbyhorses of people in the past not only by this use of your imagination, but also and primarily by solid historical research. Locate primary sources on spirits, devils, sin; immerse yourself in medieval thought. We can understand people in the past if we research intelligently and "listen" carefully.

To conclude, be careful in your interpretation of an historical event. Consider who is acting, when, before whom, and how. Notice whether your sources of information are primary or secondary, and, if the latter, remember that you are simply reading another historian's interpretation of the past, and so must consider not only the hobbyhorses of the people about whom he is writing, but also that of the historian himself. How has his interpretation been slanted by his selection and evaluation of facts? And how has your own evaluation been colored? Are you looking at the past, or at yourself?

5

The Historian
As Organizer

With your facts collected and identified, you are prepared to organize them, to shape them into a coherent vision of the past. Organizing facts gives them meaning; if we cannot relate the fact, x—x, to any other fact, then x—x has no meaning for us. But if we relate x—x to the fact of a circle, then it means something, that is, it is circular, and if we then relate it significantly to a more important fact, it not only means something, but means something significant; x—x, for example, becomes significant to the child when he learns that it can be exchanged for candy, that is, when he relates the new fact, x—x (money), to an important old fact, candy. Thus we discover meaning in our world by organizing what we see, and we understand what we see to the extent that the relationships we draw are correct: for example, if it is true that money can be exchanged for candy. Hence this chapter on organizing facts is about finding meaning in, and understanding the world we perceive.

Organization demands unity: elements in a novel are organized when they contribute to the development of a single theme; facts in an historical theory are organized when they support one conclusion. It is not enough for the historian to relate that events x, y, and z happened; he must state what these facts mean, his story must have a conclusion.

A complex conclusion is better than a simple one. A simple conclusion is reached after a brief examination of the facts; for instance, entering a classroom, you conclude that it contains a desk, many chairs, a blackboard, and other objects. Other examples of simple conclusions are the following: physicians in the sixteenth century prescribed some treatments which could have little healing effect; there were economic and political factors involved in the American Revolution.

A complex conclusion is a simple one which has been developed by asking questions and making distinctions. The simple conclusion that American colonists had economic motives for revolting from England might be developed by distinguishing the motives inciting them to revolt from those stirring them to leave England initially. If one were the first to make this distinction or comparison, he would not only be acquiring facts about the influence of economics on the colonists, but also developing a new understanding of that subject, that is, that economic motives changed, or remained the same.

I have outlined below (pp. 45–48) six steps in the organization of facts and the development of a conclusion about the past. By way of example, let us organize the facts revealed in the following five passages on prison conditions and punishment during the American Revolution:

a) Jonathan Gillett, an American captured by the British in New York, described his imprisonment in a letter to Eliza Gillett, Dec. 2, 1776:

. . . [the prisoners] are still confined and in houses where there is no fire—poor mortals, with little or no clothes—perishing with hunger, offering eight dollars in paper for one in silver to relieve there distressing hunger, occasioned for want of food. There natures are broke and gone, some almost loose there voices and some there hearing. They are crouded into churches and there guarded night and day. . . .

b) Thomas Stone, an American captured by the British, described in his "Recollections" his imprisonment in the Sugar House prison in New York:

Cold and famine were now our destiny. Not a pane of glass, nor even a board to a single window in the house, and no fire but once in three days to cook our small allowance of provision . . . Old shoes were bought and eaten with as much relish as a pig or a turkey . . . by the first of May out of sixty-nine taken with me only fifteen were alive . . . we were now attacked by a fever which threatened to clear our walls of its miserable inhabitants.

c) William Slade, an American captured by the British at Fort Washington in November, 1776, described in his diary the conditions on the British prison ship, the *Grosvenor*:

Thursday, 26th [Dec., 1776]. Last night was spent in dying grones and cries. I now gro poorly. Terrible storm as ever I saw. High wind. Drawed bisd. At noon meat and peas. Verry cold and stormey. Friday, 27th. Three men of our battalion died last night. The most melancholyest night I ever saw. Small pox increases fast.

d) Americans loyal to the British, called Loyalists, were often persecuted by the American patriots. Ann Hulton, a patriot, described in a letter to a friend the punishment of Loyalists in Boston in 1774:

. . . But the most shocking cruelty was exercised a few nights ago, upon a poor old man, a tidesman, one Malcolm . . . He was stript stark naked, one of the severest cold nights this winter, his body covered all over with tar, then with feathers, his arm dislocated in tearing off his cloaths. He was dragged in a cart with thousands attending, some beating him with clubs and knocking him out of the cart, then in again . . . These few instances amongst many serve to shew the abject state of government and the licentiousness and barbarism of the times.

e) Dr. Jonathan Potts described the American hospital at Fort George in a letter to a fellow physician, John Morgan, dated August 10, 1776:

. . . The distressed situation of the sick here is not to be described: without clothing, without bedding or a shelter sufficient to screen them from the weather . . . we have at present upwards of one thousand sick crowded into sheds and laboring under the various and cruel disorders of dysenteries, bilious putrid fevers and the effects of a confluent smallpox. . . .

1. Conclude something about your information.

You must conclude what you found, not what you hoped or expected to find. Begin, then, with the facts you have collected; place before you a small number (about 7 to 10) of your note cards with the most important information. Then simply conclude something about that information: for example, that the Church attitude toward witchcraft changed, or merely that there are a number of passages on the attitude of the Church toward witchcraft. In short, determine something your information can be shown to reveal. The preceding passages on prisons and punishment during the American Revolution provide information primarily on living conditions in British prisons during the Revolution. We will, then, develop our conclusion on that subject.

2. In developing a conclusion, begin with one passage, or a few facts.

A complex conclusion is built like a house, gradually, that is, one idea, like one brick, at a time. Begin with a single passage or a few facts. Considering only the first passage quoted above (a—p. 43), we might conclude that an American patriot imprisoned by the British reported that some American prisoners in New York were housed in churches and suffered from cold, hunger, and overcrowded conditions.

3. Identify other facts in other passages, one at a time.

We continue organizing by identifying other facts and relating them to those already established. We learn from the second passage above (b) that an American imprisoned by the British in Sugar House prison complained that the prisoners suffered and died from cold, hunger, and disease. In the third passage (c), an American on a British prison ship reveals that the prisoners were ill-fed and that many died of small-pox. The fourth passage (d) reveals that some Americans cruelly tarred and feathered their enemies, the Loyalists.

4. Determine the main point revealed by your facts.

The main point revealed in the passages cited above is that Americans in British prisons during the Revolutionary War suffered from cold, hunger, and disease. The British lacked adequate prison facilities. They converted churches, old houses, and ships into makeshift prisons. We cannot conclude that the British treatment of prisoners was less humane than the American care for prisoners, because we have no information on American prisons. And we do know that Americans did act with cruelty toward British Loyalists.

5. Develop your conclusion by making at least one distinction or comparison.

We can develop our conclusion further by making comparisons. For example, we might compare British with American prisons and discover that conditions were similar. Or we might compare prison with hospital facilities. In the fifth passage cited above (e—p. 45), we learn that men in an American hospital during the Revolution suffered from inadequate shelter and provisions. Americans could not obtain adequate provisions for their own men suffering from disease or battle-wounds. Perhaps the British likewise could not provide adequately for their own troops, much less for American prisoners. The appalling conditions in British prisons, then, might not be due to British cruelty.

A conclusion, then, can be developed in any direction by raising further questions and making additional comparisons. I have compared conditions in British prisons with those in American hospitals. You might wish to compare conditions in British prisons with those in British army camps. Make the comparisons you want to make in order to understand what you want to understand.

You should make at least one comparison of your own; do not merely locate and repeat the ideas others have developed. Comparisons can be made by identifying the main components of your subject and investigating other subjects which include both similar and contrasting elements. Examples: love in marriage compared to hate in marriage, or to love outside marriage; President John F. Kennedy/welfare policy/taxes to President Kennedy/Southeast Asian policy/taxes or to President Harry Truman/welfare policy/taxes. The point is, for example, that the relationship of Kennedy's welfare policy to taxes is determined in part by the tax revenues necessary to support his Southeast Asian policy (and by countless other factors); thus we develop our understanding of a subject by considering a multitude of related topics.

6.   Use facts supporting opposing hobbyhorses.

Your conclusion is not what you expected or hoped to find, but what you found, that is, the organization not only of those facts selected in support of a predetermined conclusion, but of all the facts related to your topic. Present both sides of controversial subjects because if you ignore your opponent's arguments, you will never understand them, and if you do not understand them, you will be able neither to refute them nor to learn from them. Thus, whether to correct the distortion in your own vision, or to persuade others of the distortions in theirs, account for all facts and viewpoints pertaining to your topic. If you do not refute other viewpoints, limit your conclusion to what you do demonstrate; e.g., conclude that an economic recession was *one* cause of declining support for higher education in California in the late 1960's (not that it was the sole cause). And do not hesitate to conclude that the facts support no single viewpoint, for this, too, is a conclusion. Your conclusion is what all the facts pertaining to your subject reveal.

6

The Historian
As Communicator

Having organized your information, you are prepared to write your paper. In writing it, you will not only be communicating, but also refining, your vision of the past. Good writing is not merely spelling correctly and placing commas in the proper spots, but rather thinking clearly and communicating effectively. The latter, at any rate, is what this chapter is about.

A. Write in your own words what you see from astride your particular hobbyhorse.

You write or speak to communicate what *you* think. Thus use words, which you select and understand, in order that you may express what you yourself have to say. Do not borrow words from scholars without making them your own: for example, do not borrow a scholar's reference to Napoleon as a tyrant unless you justify in your paper the use of this term, because if you offer no evidence that Napoleon was a tyrant, your reader will not know why you call him one, and if you have no evidence, you yourself do not know why you refer to him as one.

QUOTATIONS
It is not easy to borrow single words that will fit into the context of your paper; it is even more difficult to borrow groups

of words, that is, to use direct quotations. Do not rely on direct quotations as substitutes for your own words. For example, do not communicate your ideas on medieval beliefs about devils by quoting a contemporary historian, Lynn Thorndike:

> Lynn Thorndike, in his *History of Magic and Experimental Science*, summarized the belief of a fifteenth-century theologian in the power of devils [the italics are mine]:
>
> Peter's conception of the extent of the powers of demons is similar to *that* of our *preceding authors*. They cannot form new species in phantasy or in intellect, but they can affect the blood and humors and move bodies proportioned to themselves. That is to say, a *greater devil* of a *superior order* can move larger bodies than a minor demon and can bind his *inferior* in a stone or ring or other body . . . .

Because this quotation from Thorndike is taken out of the context of his book, the words italicized cannot be understood. Who are "Peter" and the "preceding authors," and what are "greater" and "minor" devils of "superior" and "inferior" orders? If you use a term such as "greater devil," make it your own by defining it. Only by making words your own can you communicate ideas which are clear in the context of your paper.

Use direct quotations, then, not to communicate new ideas on your subject, but to support those ideas stated in your own words. In the following passage, for example, my statement about witchcraft is supported by a quotation:

> Burchard, a German Catholic bishop, wrote in a handbook of penance in the eleventh century that Catholics believing in witchcraft should do penance (this indicated that he considered belief in witchcraft a sin):
>
> Hast thou [the penitent] believed or participated in this infidelity, that there is any woman who through certain spells and incantations can turn about the minds of men, either from hatred to love or from love to hatred, or by her bewitchments can snatch away men's goods? If thou hast believed or participated in such

acts, thou shalt do penance for one year in [*sic*] the appointed fast days.

The quotation from Burchard supports my statement that he said that Catholics believing in witchcraft should do penance, because the quotation *is* that statement.

Note that before this quotation the author, date, and source of the quotation are identified (Burchard, German bishop, eleventh century, handbook of penance); we have noted in a preceding chapter on interpretation that without such identification a statement cannot be understood. And this identification should be made *before* the quotation. Do not write the following:

It's a very funny thought that, if Bears were Bees,/ They'd build their nests at the *bottom* of trees."

The following would be better:

Winnie-the-Pooh, a bear in A. A. Milne's stories for children, sang as he climbed up a honey tree, "It's a very funny thought that, if Bears were Bees,/ They'd build their nests at the *bottom* of trees."

Limit your identification, however, to the information necessary for your reader; if you are sure that he would be familiar with Winnie-the-Pooh, omit the phrase, "a bear in A. A. Milne's stories for children."

In quoting Burchard, I have indicated also my interpretation of his statement, lest my reader conclude, for example, that Catholics in the eleventh century believed that witches stole goods, rather than what I intended to show, that belief in witchcraft was considered sinful. Since any passage yields a variety of interpretations, and since individuals will not always be struck by the same ones, the writer seeking to communicate his interpretation must state it precisely.

This interpretation should be presented before the quotation.

If I write now, after quoting Burchard, that penances were performed only on fast days, you might have to refer back to the passage (read backwards) to see if my interpretation is valid. Present your interpretations before your evidence, so that your reader can, upon reading them, see if they are supported by the ensuing evidence. In short, write backwards, that your reader may read forwards.

Present your conclusions one at a time; if you draw several conclusions from a single quotation, state them separately and support each with only that part of the quotation that provides the necessary evidence. For example, if you conclude that some Catholics in the eleventh century believed that witches stole goods, quote only the material relevant to that point: "Hast thou believed . . . that there is any woman who . . . by her bewitchments can snatch away men's goods?" In this quotation, the evidence for our conclusion is not obscured by non-essential information; deleted material is indicated by an ellipsis, that is, three spaced periods (. . .). Normally the lengthier the passage quoted, the greater is the need to omit material.

PARAPHRASING

If you use quotations to support your conclusions, you will be more likely to quote primary sources, such as the medieval Bishop Burchard's statement on witchcraft, rather than secondary ones, such as the modern historian Lynn Thorndike's summary of medieval beliefs about devils. It is usually better to paraphrase (summarize in your own words) rather than to quote directly from secondary sources. For example, I might observe that an author of another guide to research recommends that students be assigned subjects by their instructors, rather than be allowed to select their own, because he considers the process of topic selection so difficult. There is no need to quote this author directly when I can summarize his point in my own words and thus avoid the possibility of introducing words which were clear in the content of his guide, but might not be in mine. Occasionally an author will write so aptly or eloquently that his meaning will be lost unless he is quoted directly. Generally, however, you should present your line of thought in your words, rather than collect and patch together words and quotations that have not been assimilated and woven into the context of your paper. Write what you think, not merely what others have thought.

B.   Write your main conclusion, and the ideas supporting it, one at a time and in a logical sequence.

Limit your paper to a single conclusion; this is not only good organization, as noted in the preceding chapter, but it is also effective communication, because a reader can follow readily only one idea at a time. Remember how difficult it is to follow different lines of thought for a few lines, much less throughout an entire paper or book.

State your conclusion at or near the beginning of your paper, so that your reader may consider as he reads whether it is supported by your evidence. If you reserve your conclusion for the end of the paper, the reader will have to read the paper again to see how well you have supported it, since he can hardly have remembered the evidence in detail. Again, write backwards that your reader may read forwards. There are, of course, exceptions to this rule; for example, in lengthy works and for purposes of dramatic effect, part of the conclusion can be reserved for the middle or end of the presentation. The student writing a brief factual paper, however, should follow the rule, rather than the exception.

PARAGRAPHS

Each paragraph, like the entire paper, should consist of a main idea and the material necessary to support or elaborate upon it. The main idea of a paragraph should, whenever possible, be stated in the beginning of the paragraph. This idea should be a conclusion about a subject, not a statement of what the subject is: not "Let us consider the nature of the paragraph," but "The paragraph should consist of a main idea." If you write what you think about your subject, your reader will know that you are considering it.

TRANSITIONS

The ideas in support of the main conclusion of your paper should be isolated in short paragraphs which should be related carefully to one another by transitions. In the first sentence of the preceding paragraph, the phrase, "like the entire paper," is a transition; it connects a new idea ("that a *paragraph* should have a main idea") to an old idea in the preceding paragraph ("that a *paper* should have a main idea"). Relate your main idea in each paragraph to that in the preceding one. Make this transition in the first sentence of each paragraph. For example, a paragraph about dogs barking following one on difficulty in sleeping, might begin with this transition: "It is difficult to sleep [old idea] when [relationship to new idea] dogs bark all night [new idea].

SAMPLE OUTLINE OF A PAPER

The following is an outline of a paper with the conclusion stated in the beginning and the supporting points isolated in separate paragraphs and presented in a clear and logical sequence. The main point of each paragraph is stated in the first sentence; transitions between paragraphs are italicized.

First paragraph (complex conclusion in detail):

The ideal medieval student was a scholar-saint, whereas the ideal student of the Renaissance was a scholar-gentleman-citizen. The medieval student was humble, poor, and chaste, and lived in the spirit of renunciation which characterized the medieval saint; the Renaissance student was proud and sociable, delighted in secular accomplishments, and served his city-state. The medieval student used Aristotelian logic and philosophy to explain his Faith, whereas the Renaissance student used grammar and rhetoric to speak and write eloquently as a gentleman and as a servant of his city-state.

Second paragraph:

The ideal medieval student was humble. Vincent of Beauvais, a thirteenth-century educator, wrote, in *On the Education of Royal Children*, that a scholar should have "humility in knowledge." Geoffrey Chaucer, in the *Canterbury Tales*, portrayed an ideal student who was humble: [remaining information on humility].

Third paragraph:

The ideal Renaissance student was proud *rather than humble* . . . [evidence].

Fourth paragraph:

The ideal medieval student was *also* poor and chaste, renouncing worldly goods and society . . . [evidence].

Fifth paragraph:

The ideal student of the Renaissance, *on the contrary,* was friendly and sociable, *delighting in society's attractions* . . . [evidence].

Sixth paragraph:

The medieval student, *finally,* studied Aristotelian logic and philosophy, which he used to support his Faith . . . [evidence].

Seventh paragraph:

The student of the Renaissance, *on the other hand, studied* grammar and rhetoric, that he might speak and write eloquently as a gentleman and servant of his city-state . . . [evidence].

Eighth paragraph:

To conclude, although some scholars have observed that Chaucer's ideal student, quiet and dedicated to learning, characterizes ideal students of all eras, he is typically medieval. Contrasting medieval and Renaissance purposes for education produced differing descriptions of ideal students.

TOPICAL ORGANIZATION

The organization in this paper on the ideal medieval student is topical (according to the nature of the subject):

medieval humility (paragraph 2)/Renaissance pride (3)/medieval renunciation (4)/Renaissance sociability (5)/medieval study of logic and philosophy (6)/Renaissance study of rhetoric and grammar (7).

This topical organization is better than the following chronological one (according to time—medieval, followed by Renaissance):

medieval humility/medieval renunciation/medieval study of *logic* and *philosophy*/

Renaissance pride/Renaissance sociability/Renaissance study of *grammar* and *rhetoric.*

In this chronological organization, when the reader learns that the medieval scholar studied logic and philosophy, he will wonder what was studied in the Renaissance; then, discovering much later in the paper that rhetoric and grammar were studied, he will have to turn back to an earlier page to review the comparison in detail.

Topical organization clarifies for the reader what he does not know, e.g., medieval humility contrasts with Renaissance pride. Chronological organization brings out what the reader already knows, e.g., that the Renaissance followed the Middle Ages. Organize your ideas, not mechanically, by chronology, geography, and so forth, but personally, by the manner in which you shaped them, that is, by the distinctions you drew in developing your conclusion, e.g., the distinction between humility and pride in scholars of two different periods of history. Chronological order, of course, should be maintained within your topical arrangement. For example, *within* the topical organization of material on ecology (water pollution/air pollution/noise pollution), chronological order should be maintained (water pollution, 1960's/ water pollution, 1970's/ air pollution, 1960's/ air pollution, 1970's/ noise pollution, 1960's/ noise pollution, 1970's).

ORGANIZATION OF SUBJECTS DIAGRAMED

Note the following example of organization of the subject, theological attitudes toward women:

i) Poor organization—theological attitudes toward women

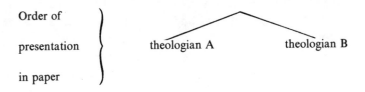

Order of

presentation

in paper

[The organization in the above diagram (i) does not clarify for the reader the specific characteristics of the attitudes of theologians A and B toward women.]

ii) Improved organization—theological attitudes toward women

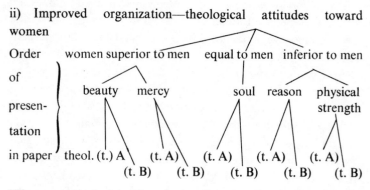

Order of presentation in paper

[The organization in the above diagram (ii) clarifies for the reader the characteristics of the attitudes of theologians A and B toward women. The facts in the paper represented by this diagram are more carefully organized and hence would be better understood than the facts, largely unorganized, in the paper represented by the first diagram.]

C. Write for your reader.

Although you might, as has been urged, present a single conclusion in your own words, supported with ideas presented in a logical sequence, you could still make it difficult for your reader to understand you. A reference to a double-screen, for example, might bewilder those unfamiliar with basketball; so use words which both you and your reader understand. The audience for your paper is your instructor, or any educated individual. Do not use slang or the jargon of a particular vocation or class of society; use words which are the common possession of all classes. Your instructor might not know the meaning of some of the words you use, just as you might not know the meaning of terms such as "docent," which is a popular word in educational circles.

In writing for your audience, consider the following suggestions.

1. IDENTIFY TERMS

Identify terms that might not be readily understood. Educated people will recognize Santa Claus, Napoleon, Julius Caesar, and witchcraft, but perhaps not Burchard, handbooks of penance, and the Battle of Poitiers. Identify obscure terms with a phrase, as has been done in our discussion of Burchard (a German Catholic bishop in the eleventh century).

Terms central to your subject and capable of yielding different meanings should also be identified. For example, if you write about witchcraft, mysticism, or liberalism, define those terms (are you discussing witchcraft as a religion, or as a superstition?). Dictionaries are useful, since they list all the meanings, from which you can choose the one related to your subject.

2. OMIT BACKGROUND INFORMATION

Although you should identify obscure terms in a few phrases and important topics in a few sentences or a paragraph, do not include additional background material in your paper. If your reader desires background on witchcraft, he can consult encyclopedias or other books; your paper is what he cannot locate elsewhere, that is, what you think about witchcraft. Minimize background material and proceed to your conclusion and its support.

3. WRITE CLEAR SENTENCES

Awkward sentences, vague terms and other characteristics of poor writing force your reader to piece together your meaning: Who is Burchard? What is the writer's interpretation of this quotation? What is "something"? If your meaning, on the other hand, is immediately clear, your reader can consider more important questions, such as whether this bishop's attitude would have been the same as the attitudes of other bishops. Free

your reader's mind from the former questions that he may
consider the latter. The more effectively you write, the more
intelligently you enable your reader to read.

A sentence, like a paragraph or paper, should contain one
main idea. Break down lengthy, awkward sentences into short,
simple ones.

> Poor: A sentence should have one main idea and spell your
> words correctly, which helps your reader follow what you
> write. [How does spelling correctly help your reader
> follow better what is written? What is the subject of
> "spell"? To what does "which" refer?]
>
> Better: A sentence should have one main idea, so that a reader
> can focus his attention upon it. The reader's attention
> should not be distracted by misspelled words.

Sentences, like paragraphs, should be linked by transitions.
Note the following transitions: The boy hit the *ball*. The *ball*
soared deep into *centerfield*. The *centerfielder* raced toward the
fence and *snared the ball*. That *catch* saved the game for the
fourth graders and enabled them to advance to the finals of the
school tournament. *However, they* were not to win the next
game.

Words and phrases within your sentences should also be
properly linked. Do not write "the boy hit the ball chewing
gum," but "the boy chewing gum hit the ball." And do not write,
"I am also hungry," but, "I also am hungry," unless you mean
that you are *also hungry* (in addition to being thirsty) rather than
that *you also* (in addition to your friends) are hungry. Place
adverbs and adjectives, whether words or phrases, next to the
words they modify.

4. ELIMINATE UNNECESSARY WORDS

You will digest this guide to research much faster if it is 150
rather than 300 pages long; unnecessary words should always be

eliminated. The following material can be eliminated from a paper: a) paragraphs not necessary to support or clarify the main conclusion: b) repeated words or ideas; c) words not pertaining to the subject of the paper, such as remarks about your research and writing ("After a good deal of research I have come to the conclusion that the Church opposed witchcraft" equals "The Church opposed witchcraft"; the reader is aware that you conducted research and that you write what you think); d) words with little meaning ("Many *other* words *really* don't *actually* add *anything of value* to the meaning of a sentence *after all on account of the fact that* they are redundant or meaningless" equals "Many words do not add to the meaning of a sentence since they are redundant or meaningless"). It is sometimes helpful to circle the essential words in a rough draft and then to write a revised draft in shorter, simpler sentences. Or try crossing out as many words as you can without changing or obscuring your meaning.

5. BE PRECISE

If you are not certain that Napoleon was a tyrant, do not call him one; call him Napoleon. Clarify or delete vague ideas, such as "et cetera" or "something." Do not write that "the book said," "the institution decreed," or "the empire was tired," for books do not talk, institutions do not issue decrees, and empires do not become fatigued. Select your words carefully, use a dictionary, state the truth, be precise.

D. Footnotes, punctuation for quotations, and bibliography.

Ideas are personal visions developed by individual thinkers; authors deserve credit for their ideas, just as architects do for their designs. Identify in footnotes and a bibliography the sources for your ideas, so that your reader may distinguish those you developed from those you collected. It is one thing to find ideas in one or two encyclopedia articles, and another to develop them from material in thirty books on a variety of subjects. The identification of your sources also enables your reader to investigate your subject further, if he so desires.

1.   Footnotes

A footnote is a reference or statement at the bottom of a page, the end of a chapter or the end of a book. The following statement is footnoted at the bottom of this page: An Englishman, William Merlee, based weather predictions on the activity of fleas.[1] In general, footnotes should be used when you are quoting or paraphrasing primary or secondary sources, presenting little-known facts, or referring to theories not widely accepted. Footnotes should also be used occasionally to indicate the principal sources for general information. Footnotes may be typed either at the bottom of each page or in a single list at the end of the paper.

FIRST FOOTNOTE REFERENCES

The following are samples of the most common types of footnotes; titles of books, magazines, and newspapers are underlined (italicized in print), and titles of chapters or articles in books, magazines, or newspapers are placed in quotation marks:

a)   A one volume book by a single author
 [1] Christopher Dawson, *Religion and the Rise of Western Culture,* p. 181.

b)   A work of more than one volume or by more than one author
 [2] M. Félibien and G. Lobineau, *Histoire de la ville de Paris,* IV, 100.

c)   A chapter or section written by one author in a work edited by another (e.g., a collection of essays or primary sources)

1. A. C. Crombie, *Medieval and Early Modern Science,* I, *Science in the Middle Ages: V–XIII Centuries,* p. 99.

³A. L. Gabriel, "The College System in the Fourteenth Century Universities," in *Forward Movement of the Fourteenth Century,* ed. Francis Lee Utley, p. 81.
⁴John Locke, *An Essay Concerning Human Understanding,* in John Beatty and Oliver Johnson, *Heritage of Western Civilization,* 2nd ed., p. 142.

d) One book quoted in another
⁵James Boswell, *Life of Johnson,* April 16, 1775, cited in F. W. Bateson, *A Guide to English Literature,* p. 103.

e) Articles in periodicals
⁶ Paul Vanderwood, "Genesis of the Rurales: Mexico's Early Struggle for Public Security," *The Hispanic American Historical Review,* L [volume no.], No. 2 (May 1970), 323.

f) Well-known sources with formal divisions
⁷ William Shakespeare, *Hamlet,* I, i, 4.
⁸Aristotle, *The Nicomachean Ethics,* X, i.

If a bibliography (see below, p. 66) is not required for your paper, the first reference to a source should include complete bibliographical information—for example, not only the author and title of a work, but also the place, publisher and date of publication (in parentheses):

¹ Wallace K. Ferguson, *Europe in Transition: 1300–1520* (Boston: Houghton Mifflin Company, 1962), p. 81.

SUBSEQUENT FOOTNOTE REFERENCES

The second and subsequent times you refer in a footnote to a particular work, give only the last name of the author and the page number:

¹ Dawson, p. 179.

Another method of identifying works cited in previous footnotes requires the use of the Latin abbreviations ibid., op. cit., and loc. cit. Ibid. (short for *ibidem,* meaning "in the same place") is used when you refer to a source cited in the footnote immediately preceding:

¹J. C. Furnas, *The Americans: A Social History of the United States, 1587–1914,* p. 100.
²ibid., p. 105.
³ibid., p. 108.

Op. cit. (short for *opere citato*—"in the work cited") is used when one refers to a book cited previously, but not in the footnote immediately preceding:

[1] J. C. Furnas, *The Americans: A Social History of the United States, 1587–1914,* p. 110.
[2] G. G. Coulton, *Social Life in Britain from the Conquest to the Reformation,* p. 127.
[3] Furnas, op. cit., p. 112.

Loc. cit. (*loco citato*—"in the place cited") is used when you refer to the same passage of a work cited in a recent footnote. Scholars today, instead of using op. cit. and loc. cit., favor the simpler method of citing the author's last name and the page number of his work (Sterne, p. 82).

Other abbreviations and Latin terms used frequently are ca. or c. ("about"), cf. or cp. ("compare"), e.g. ("for example"), i.e. ("that is"), viz. ("namely"), and passim ("here and there"). Passim indicates that the information cited in a footnote can be found almost anywhere in a particular work ("here and there"), rather than on specific pages:

[1] On methods of investigation in medieval science, see A. C. Crombie, *Medieval and Early Modern Science,* I, *Science in the Middle Ages: V–XIII Centuries,* passim.

2.   Punctuation of quotations

Quotations of 100 words or more should be indented—set in from both right and left margins—and should not be enclosed in quotation marks. Unless your quotation is an integral part of your sentence, introduce it with a statement followed by a colon, as in the following example:

Burchard, a German Catholic bishop, wrote in a handbook of penance in the eleventh century that Catholics believing in witchcraft should do penance:

Hast thou [the penitent] believed or participated in this infidelity, that there is any woman
who through certain spells and incantations can

> turn about the minds of men, either from
> hatred to love or from love to hatred, or by her
> bewitchments can snatch away men's goods? If
> thou hast believed or participated in such acts,
> thou shalt do penance for one year in [*sic*] the
> appointed fast days.

Note that unclear words in the quotation above have been explained in brackets: "thou [the penitent]." Always use brackets when inserting in quoted material your own clarification of that material. For example, quotations inadequately punctuated can be clarified for the reader by the insertion, in brackets, of the appropriate punctuation ("Was he hungry [?]"). If the punctuation, spelling, or content of a quotation, seems to be in error, the Latin term *sic* ("thus") should be inserted in brackets to indicate to the reader that the quotation has been copied accurately. In the above quotation, for example, the original source does read "in," not "on."

Quotations of fewer than 100 words should be typed as part of the text (not indented) and enclosed in quotation marks. Periods and commas are always placed inside double quotation marks:

> "As for me," said Patrick Henry, "give me liberty or give me death."

Colons and semicolons are always placed outside double quotation marks:

> King George's opinion on the dispute with the colonists was that "blows must decide"; he ruled out all compromise.

Question marks and exclamation points are placed outside quotation marks if an entire sentence is a question or exclamation, and inside them if only the quoted material is a question or exclamation:

> Patrick Henry asked, "Is this the part of wise men, engaged in a great and arduous struggle for liberty?"

> But how many colonists would say with Henry, "Give me liberty or give me death"?

The number for a footnote is placed at the end of the material cited and after all punctuation:

> Geoffrey Gorer has noted that Americans believe in the "magical health-giving virtues of certain foods." [1]

3.   Bibliography

The bibliography is a list of the books, articles, and other sources of information used in preparing your paper. You should have two lists, one of primary and the other of secondary sources; each should be arranged alphabetically by the last name of the author. Sources included in the bibliography need not have been cited in a footnote, but should have added to your knowledge of your subject. Note the following sample bibliographical entries.

Primary Sources

Coulton, G. G., ed. *Social Life in Britain from the Conquest to the Reformation.* Cambridge: University Press, 1918, reprint, New York: Barnes and Noble, Inc., 1968 [a collection of sources].

Sterne, Laurence. *The Life and Opinions of Tristram Shandy, Gentleman.* Ed. James Aiken Work. New York: The Odyssey Press, 1940.

Secondary Sources

Albright, William F. *Archaeology, Historical Analogy, and Early Biblical Tradition.* Baton Rouge: Louisiana State University Press, 1966.

Jones, Howard Mumford. *O Strange New World. American Culture: The Formative Years.* London: Chatto and Windus, 1965.

CHAPTER 7

The Historian
In The Present

The historian strives to understand people in the past that he may better understand himself and his society. We have traced in Chapters Two through Six the development of our conclusions about the past; let us consider in this final chapter our conclusions about ourselves and our society. What, in short, is the ultimate meaning of our experiences as historians?

1.   Has your research either confirmed or altered your understanding of yourself, your society, or mankind?

Ideally, the historian does not merely acquire facts about the past, but rather develops a new interpretation or understanding of reality, past and present. This new understanding might be a deepening conviction that man has not changed greatly in the past two thousand years; such was the conclusion of the eminent British historian, Kenneth Clarke, in the summation of his book, *Civilisation.* The historian faces a multitude of similarly fascinating questions about himself, his society, and mankind: Are men motivated primarily by desire for material or spiritual gain? Am I myself motivated by desire for material or spiritual gain? Are great men chiefly the creators or the products of history? Is man inherently good or evil?

Let us consider how the study of the ideal medieval student

(outlined in Chapter Six) might lead us to a better understanding of American society in 1970. We concluded that the ideal medieval student was a scholar-saint, whereas the ideal student of the Renaissance was a scholar-gentleman-citizen. In striving to understand educational developments within American society in 1970, we might compare the ideal student of 1960 with one of 1970, and conclude that the former was a scholar-businessman-pillar of society, whereas the latter was a scholar-social worker-hobo. Students in 1960 enrolled in courses such as business, engineering, and home economics, and joined fraternities or sororities, in preparation for careers which would provide economic security and social respectability. Students in 1970, on the other hand, enrolled in courses such as sociology, psychology, and art, and dressed casually or even carelessly, in preparation for careers which would offer human rather than materialistic involvement, whether in serving underprivileged classes as social workers, or in expressing themselves in art. If we reflect upon these contrasting ideals (businessman vs. social worker), and recall the theory of the double truth, we might conclude that although we had planned to become social workers, there might be some value in becoming businessmen, if only to acquire the capital with which to effect major social reforms. Thus, as a consequence of our historical inquiries, we might act differently (e.g., take courses in business administration and become businessmen) or at least see our world differently (e.g., be more aware of contemporary developments in education).

2. How does your world look when you use historical thinking?

Through the use of this guide you have not only developed a vision of the past which might alter *what* you think in the present, but you have also utilized an historical manner of thinking about the past, which might alter *how* you think about the present. Can you use historical thinking (hobbyhorse sense) to understand better not only people in the past, but also yourself and your friends in the present?

I could cite one million, forty-eight thousand, six hundred and eighteen examples of the lack of understanding and communication which has resulted as a consequence of the scarcity of hobbyhorse sense. You need not tremble and quake, however; I shall cite only four.

a) People assume incorrectly that others with different experiences know precisely what they themselves know, and hence they fail to communicate effectively because they do not realize the need to identify their terms (e.g., a student in my class, assuming that her audience knew what tarot cards were, did not identify them, and was amazed to discover that only four of the twenty-five members of her audience knew what she had been talking about).

b) People do not respect others with whose viewpoints they differ sharply.(Graduate students in political science at a leading university are said to have voted against the hiring of one of the foremost politicians of the twentieth century simply because they did not approve of his political activities. Lacking a respect for this politician's rare knowledge and talents, the students declined to hire him as a consequence of their intellectual prejudices, which are no more justifiable than religious, national, class, race, or any other type of prejudice.)

c) Individuality is seldom encouraged (a citizen is prohibited from painting pictures on the sidewalk in front of his business establishment).

d) People frequently do not consult and interpret carefully primary sources (they judge others without gathering the facts necessary to support their evaluations; for example, they conclude that the city officials intolerantly prohibited the storekeeper from painting on the sidewalk in front of his store, without asking the officials themselves for their justification of the prohibition).

What I am saying, in short, is that people, including historians, including myself, frequently do not demonstrate the training in historical thinking which is necessary for understanding, communication, and love.

3. What use can you make of your skills in writing and in using the library?

You might in the future buy a house, write a novel, travel to Europe, play football on the beach, become a nurse, secretary, engineer, or journalist; what use will there be in such endeavors for the skills which you have developed in writing and in using the library? In the case of library skills, if you buy a house, write a novel, travel to Europe, or play football, remember that there are guides for these activities. If you desire to do something well, you can locate in a library the most respected authorities on the subject which interests you. Constance Winchell's *Guide to Reference Books* is one book through which authorities in any field can be located.

Your understanding of the process by which an idea is developed can be used when you read books, that is, the ideas developed by others. Read Appendix II in which it has been suggested how you can read more intelligently by applying what you have learned in writing your paper.

4. Create your present world as you recreated the past.

Just as historians develop different interpretations or visions of the past, so people develop different visions of the present; you see one world, I see another. It is easiest to accept that vision which our particular circumstances, generation, or society make most readily available to us. I suggest, however, that you be an individual, that you carry your own lantern, that you develop your vision of the present just as you developed your vision of the past. Select and arrange the facts of your world in your own way—question, analyze, search. You can create your own world, and although you cannot change the world, you can change the way you see the world; you can change the world which you see.

Let us take the differing worlds created by two housewives, Jill and Jan, in similar circumstances. Jan might see a day of boring and trivial chores, such as preparing her husband's breakfast, doing laundry, and changing diapers. Jill might have the same chores, but see them as opportunities to express her love for her children and husband. Furthermore, Jill might see a few hours during her day as opportunities to engage in entertaining or meaningful activities, such as sewing, gardening, or reading. I am suggesting neither that one choose to be a housewife nor that one enjoy changing diapers. My point is that Jill is committed to something, that she has found significance in her activities. We can make our worlds significant merely by *choosing* to do so.

A successful college basketball coach considers the building of character important; he sees his role as developing not only basketball players, but also men. I esteem the values of individuality, humility, and understanding; hence I characterize the historian as one who humbles himself in an attempt to understand the viewpoints of his fellow men and thus extend his individual understanding of reality. But the basketball coach is not building the character of his players, nor am I inspiring in my students a sense of their individuality and a concern for their fellow man; we are both simply riding our hobbyhorses in our own imaginary worlds, while our players and students are cursing us in their sleep or laughing at us in the halls. Or truer yet, they are not giving us a thought. And that is my point. The rest of the world does not care. But I do. I shall be whatever I choose to be. I am what I think I am. And that is all that I am asking of you: to care about yourself, to choose to be something, and to be it. Build your own hobbyhorse, and ride it. The world may laugh at you, but the world itself is on a funny hobbyhorse.

Appendix I: **Bibliography**

Having urged students to use guides in locating authoritative works on subjects of interest, I shall refer them to Winchell's *Guide to Reference Books* and the AHA's *Guide to Historical Literature* for bibliographical material. Included in the following bibliography, however, are a few works supplementing material presented in this guide.

A. Guides to reference books and to history (discussed in Chapter Three of this guide)

Winchell, Constance M. *Guide to Reference Books.* 8th ed. Chicago: American Library Association, 1967. Two supplements have been published.

Walford, A. J. *Guide to Reference Material.* 2nd ed. London: The Library Association, volumes I (*Science and Technology,* asst. eds., K. R. Rider and F. R. Taylor, 1966), II (*Philosophy & Psychology, Religion, Social Sciences, Geography, Biography & History,* asst. eds., A. L. Smyth and C. A. Toase, 1968), and III (*Generalities, Languages, The Arts, and Literature,* 1970). [Walford's work is the standard guide to reference material in British libraries—it is useful also for American libraries.]

The American Historical Association's *Guide to Historical Literature.* George Frederick Howe, chairman, Board of Editors. New York: The Macmillan Company, 1961.

Handlin, Oscar, et. al., eds. *Harvard Guide to American History.* Cambridge, Mass.: Harvard Univ. Press, Belknap Press, 1954.

B. Guides and bibliographies for disciplines other than history

1. ART
   Chamberlin, M. W. *Guide to Art Reference Books.* Chicago: American Library Association, 1959.
2. ENGLISH LITERATURE
   Bateson, F. W. *A Guide to English Literature.* 2nd ed. London: Longmans, 1967.
   The Cambridge Bibliography of English Literature. Ed. F. W. Bateson. Cambridge: University Press, 1940. 3 vols. and index. Supplement, 1957.

3. PHILOSOPHY

Copleston, F. C. *A History of Philosophy.* London: Burns, Oates and Washbourne, 1947–66, 8 vols.

4. RELIGION

Encyclopedia of Religion and Ethics. Edited by J. Hastings, with the assistance of J. A. Selbie and other scholars. New York: Scribner, 1908–26, 12 vols. and index.

New Catholic Encyclopedia. Editorial staff at the Catholic University of America. New York: McGraw-Hill, 1967. 15 vols.

Universal Jewish Encyclopedia. Ed. Isaac Landman. New York: Universal Jewish Encyclopedia, Inc., 1939–44. 10 vols. and reading guide and index.

5. SCIENCE, HISTORY OF

Sarton, George. *A Guide to the History of Science; A First Guide for the Study of the History of Science With Introductory Essays on Science and Tradition.* New York: The Ronald Press Co., 1952.

"Critical Bibliography of the History and Philosophy of Science and of the History of Civilization," in *Isis.* Cambridge, Mass.: History of Science Society, 1913– v. 1, no. 1– [from June, 1955, entitled "Critical Bibliography of the History of Science and its Cultural Influences"].

6. SOCIAL SCIENCES

White, Carl M. and associates. *Sources of Information in the Social Sciences: A Guide to the Literature.* Totowa, N.J.: The Bedminster Press, 1964.

C. Guides to research

Barzun, Jacques, and Henry F. Graff. *The Modern Researcher.* New York: Harcourt, Brace, and World, 1970.

D. Philosophy of history

Collingwood, Robin George. *The Idea of History.* Oxford: Clarendon Press, 1946.

Meyerhoff, Hans, ed. *The Philosophy of History in our Time.* Garden City, New York: Doubleday, 1959.

E. Introduction to history

Nevins, Allan. *The Gateway to History.* Revised Anchor Books edition, Garden City, N.Y.: Doubleday and Co., Inc., by arrangement with D. C. Heath and Co., 1962.

F. English usage

Baker, Sheridan. *The Practical Stylist.* New York: Thomas Y. Crowell Company, 1962.
Strunk, William, and E. B. White. *The Elements of Style*, 2nd ed. New York: Macmillan, 1972.

G. Style manuals (documentation and preparation of papers)

A Manual of Style, 11th ed. Chicago and London: Univ. of Chicago Press, 1969.
MLA Style Sheet. 2nd ed. New York: The Modern Language Association, 1970.

Appendix II: **Reading History**

Since reading history is identifying and analyzing what an historian has written, he who has had the experience of writing history is prepared to read more intelligently. In this appendix it is suggested how the guidelines provided in this book can be applied when reading historical works.

How to choose what to read.

Although in college you are usually assigned reading material, you should know how to locate appealing and authoritative books on your own. Authoritative works on historical subjects can be located in the American Historical Association's *Guide to Historical Literature* (see above, p. 24), which includes books published before 1961 (up to about 1957–1960). Similar guides, such as Bateson's *Guide to English Literature*, are available for many other disciplines and can be located in Constance Winchell's *Guide to Reference Books* (see above, p. 25). Books can be located also by browsing among appealing sections of the library (systematic browsing, pp. 27–33) or by asking authorities, such as teachers.

You can locate entertaining or relevant books by following the guidelines in Chapter Two for the selection of a subject for research; identify significant experiences, interests, and goals, and draw from these a reading program combining several aims or interests.

A reading program can be more flexible than a research assignment. You might survey Western Civilization, investigate the history of a city, or dabble in folklore and ancient maps. Before you begin to read, it helps to outline a reading plan and spend an afternoon locating the best books available on your subject, since it is better to select the most appealing seven or eight books from forty examined than to locate only one and begin reading.

Outline in your notes the vision of the past that you develop from your reading; relate the books to one another as you related facts in writing your paper. What is the relationship between American and European history? What is the role of institutions in human affairs? Why are wars fought? Organize your reading around your interests, questions, and goals. Are you an economic, political, or social historian? Are you a Diogenes searching for an honest man, or an entertainer collecting stories and trivia? Shape your vision of the past around yourself.

How to read.

Reading, it has been noted, is identifying and analyzing the process by which an author has developed an idea or conclusion. What subject did he select (Chapter Two of this guide); what types of sources did he consult (Chapter Three); how did he interpret and organize his material (Chapters Four and Five); and how did he communicate his conclusion (Chapter Six)? Like history, reading involves people: one person on his hobbyhorse (the reader) striving to understand another person on his hobbyhorse (the author). The serious reader is interested not merely in facts, but in people and in how, as individuals, they have selected and shaped their material.

Consider the reading of an article, "The Historical Roots of Our Ecologic Crisis," by Lynn White (from *Science*, 10 March 1967, vol. 155, no. 3767). This article is reprinted in part C of this appendix (pp. 84 ff.).

Identify the subject matter of your reading material and consider what you might write about it.

The subject of the article "The Historical Roots of our Ecologic Crisis" is, simply, the historical roots of our alleged ecologic crisis. Might these roots or causes be factories and automobiles, or perhaps the entire Industrial Revolution? What might you write about the crisis—that it should be met with more advanced technology, such as better smog-control devices? Identify the subject of your reading material from its title, preface, introduction, or opening paragraphs, and consider your perspective, that is, what you might write on that subject. When we have a perspective on a topic, when we know something about it, we read more attentively; athletes enjoy sports magazines, farmers agricultural periodicals, professors scholarly journals or magazines about their hobbies.

You can even have a perspective on subjects you know nothing about. Before reading a history of a war, for example, you might consider whether economic, political, or religious issues are most likely to cause wars. If you have no information about this particular war, consider the causes of your neighborhood street fights or family quarrels. If you reflect that people usually fight over money, and then read that a war had a tremendous impact upon the religious values of a society, the author's perspective on warfare (religious consequences) will be highlighted by comparison with your perspective (economic causes). Furthermore, realizing that you have been looking at wars from a limited perspective (economic causes), you might re-evaluate the significance of the war in Vietnam, or your fights with your sister, by considering the religious or other consequences of these struggles. Some students, unfortunately, identify neither the author's perspective nor their own on the subject matter of their reading material; hence they neither appreciate what an author does with his subject nor learn anything about themselves.

The point, then, is that Lynn White does not attribute the ecologic crisis to automobiles and factories. What *is* his perspective? We are now prepared to read with anticipation and to appreciate Lynn White's search for something we had not even considered, that is, the deeper causes for our crisis, the historical roots beneath the surface.

Identify the thesis and argument.

Read not merely for information but for an author's conclusion about his subject (his thesis) and its support (his argument). Each chapter or section of a work contains a single point which is an integral part of the author's thesis and argument. These points are frequently made at the beginning or end of a chapter, or are otherwise indicated by subheadings, italics, or writing style (e.g., "above all," "to summarize," or "therefore we must conclude that"). The relationship of all parts of a work to its main subject or thesis must be understood. For example, we understand why Lynn White mentioned democracy in his article on the ecologic crisis only if we can explain how he related it to the crisis. The following summary of Lynn White's article (presented predominantly in his own words) illustrates how you can read for an author's thesis and argument rather than merely for information.

Problem: Individual proposals for the solution of our ecologic crisis (e.g., ban the bomb, tear down billboards) seem too partial, too negative. Let us clarify our thinking by considering the historical roots of the crisis.

Thesis: Christianity is partially responsible for our ecologic crisis because her doctrine of man's supremacy over nature has encouraged an attitude of indifference toward our environment. We must rethink our attitude toward nature.

Thesis in more detail, with support (a through h):

a) The ecologic crisis is the result of the marriage of science and technology in the mid-nineteenth century with the widespread acceptance of the Baconian creed that science is technological control over nature. Prior democratic revolutions had made this marriage possible by reducing social barriers and thus asserting a functional unity of brain (science, which had been aristocratic, speculative, and intellectual) and hand (technology, which had been lower-class, empirical, and action-oriented).

b) Modern technology and science, whose marriage led to our crisis, are products of Western (rather than Eastern) civilization. Their leadership in the West begins not in the seventeenth and eighteenth centuries (with the Scientific and Industrial Revolutions), but rather in the Middle Ages (fourteenth-century scientists, windmill, water wheel, weight-driven mechanical clock, etc.).

c) Since both our scientific and technological movements originated and achieved world dominance in the Middle Ages, it seems that we cannot understand their nature and their present impact unless we examine fundamental medieval assumptions and developments.

d) Medieval man became an exploiter of nature (by the end of the seventh century some northern European peasants were using heavy plows rather than light Roman scratch plows. To pull these new plows, they had to pool their oxen; thus they became exploiters of nature with power-driven machines). Ninth-century Frankish calendar illuminations, depicting men plowing, harvesting, chopping trees, and otherwise "coercing" nature, reveal the new exploitive attitude towards nature.

e) This new attitude was perhaps the result of an application of the Judeo-Christian teaching that God created nature for man's benefit (man was above nature, created in the image of God, and given dominion over all creatures). By destroying pagan animism (the belief that spirits dwelled in nature), Christianity enabled men to exploit nature in a mood of indifference to the feelings of natural objects.

f) The Christian doctrine of man's supremacy over nature led to technological advances in the Latin West rather than the Greek East for two reasons: first, Western theology was voluntarist rather than intellectual (Latins believed that salvation was to be attained by acting rightly, whereas Greeks believed it was to be attained by perceiving the truth correctly, and thus the conquest of Nature would emerge more easily in the Western atmosphere of acting rather than the Eastern one of contemplating); second, natural theology in the West from the thirteenth century on became the effort to understand God by discovering how his creation operates (a scientific approach), whereas natural theology in the East remained the effort to discover religious truths symbolized by nature (an artistic approach).

g) Since modern science is an extrapolation of natural theology and since modern technology is at least partly to be explained as a voluntarist, Occidental realization of the Christian dogma of man's rightful mastery over nature, and since the marriage of science and technology have led to our ecologic crisis, Christianity bears a huge burden of guilt for this crisis.

h) To meet the crisis, we must change our attitude toward nature. The medieval St. Francis of Assisi tried to substitute the idea of the equality of all creatures for the idea of man's limitless rule of creation; when we rethink our attitude toward nature, St. Francis may point a direction.

Criticize the thesis.

A thesis is sound if additional facts cannot be cited to disprove or qualify it, if interpretations are convincing, and if relationships between facts are correct.

Additional facts can be cited to qualify White's thesis. He wrote that "Christianity bears a huge burden of guilt" for our ecologic crisis, but he did not account for the Christian doctrine of the vanity of the world, which might diminish that guilt; Christians renouncing the world do not coerce nature in order to make bigger castles, larger factories, faster cars, more destructive bombs.

Some of Lynn White's interpretations are not convincing. Why should man's attitude toward nature change with the development of a heavier plow in the early Middle Ages (passage d above, p. 79), rather than with the invention of agriculture, the wheel, gunpowder, the airplane, or the hydrogen bomb? White observes that the new attitude toward nature is reflected in Frankish calendar illuminations depicting men plowing, harvesting, chopping trees, and otherwise "coercing" nature (the months had been illustrated previously by passive personifications). But a picture on a calendar is a picture on a calendar, not a philosophical statement of one's attitude toward nature; a picture on a calendar proves that someone drew the picture, that the things represented in the picture were known, not necessarily that whoever drew the picture was expressing a new attitude that man was justified in coercing nature.

The relationships drawn by White are not always convincing, either. He argues that the marriage of science and technology in the nineteenth century led to our ecologic crisis, that science and technology "originated" and achieved "world dominance" in the Middle Ages, and that therefore it seems that we must understand the medieval assumptions underlying science and technology if we are to understand their present impact. But why is it medieval assumptions in particular that should be understood? Why not the assumptions underlying Greek science? And since our ecologic crisis is allegedly a product of the merger of science and technology in the nineteenth century with the acceptance of the Baconian creed that science is technological control over nature, why not examine nineteenth (and eighteenth and seventeenth) century assumptions?

Many criticisms of White's thesis could be made, but the point is simply that the reader should identify and critically analyze his argument.

Identify the author and his perspective.

Reading is not only identifying and analyzing a thesis and an argument, but also understanding how a *person* has shaped his material, how he sees his subject. Lynn White writes that once, in a conversation with Aldous Huxley, he interrupted to point out that "the rabbit itself had been brought as a domestic animal to England in 1176, presumably to improve the protein diet of the peasantry." Who would interrupt with such a comment? Hardly a policeman, lawyer, or nurse. The references throughout the article to historical, medieval, scientific, technological, and religious facts suggest that the author rides a history-of-science-and-technology as well as religious hobbyhorse. His individual subject is ecology/history/medieval science and technology/ Christianity. He is, in fact, a professor of history at the University of California at Los Angeles, specializing in medieval science and technology, and with training in Christian theology. Although some may doubt that a professor of medieval science and technology could solve our ecologic crisis, Lynn White does offer a unique perspective on the subject, and we can enjoy watching him ingeniously riding his hobbyhorse into the past. And, as we shall see in our final evaluation, perhaps he *does* have a point.

Consider your own hobbyhorse.

Noting the doctrine of man's supremacy over nature, Lynn White argues that Christianity shares a huge burden of guilt for our ecologic crisis; pointing to the doctrine of the vanity of the world, I have suggested (p. 80) that it does not. It would be easy to pursue our disagreement. Lynn White might note that the doctrine of the vanity of the world is simply a variation of the doctrine of man's supremacy over nature: man is important, the world is not. I might reply that the doctrine of man's supremacy over nature does not necessitate an indifference toward it; nature can still be revered and protected as a thing of beauty and as part of God's handiwork.

But suppose Lynn White and I, recognizing the limitations of our perspectives, should strive to understand one another by applying the principle of the double truth (see above, p. 12): perhaps the doctrine of man's supremacy has led some to be indifferent to nature; maybe the doctrine of the vanity of the world has curbed the greed of others. Perhaps Lynn White and I can agree to some extent.

Our agreement, however, would only raise more questions. How has Christianity influenced man's attitude toward nature, considering *all* her doctrines? *Who* has been influenced by Christianity to coerce nature, and *when?* Perhaps not "Christianity" or all Christians, perhaps only certain interpreters of Christianity are to blame for our ecologic crisis. Possibly Deism or Materialism or Human Nature have led some to interpret Christian doctrine as justifying the coercion of nature. If Lynn White and I do not persist in defending our personal, limited perspectives on Christianity and the ecologic crisis, we may resolve our differences and approach the whole truth.

Render a final judgment on the merit of an author's work.

To conclude that an author wrote this or misinterpreted that or did not account for something else is not necessarily to render an intelligent judgment of a work. Let us consider first what we cannot conclude about Lynn White's article.

We cannot conclude that an article is dull or uninteresting, but only that it does not interest us, and since it was not written to interest you or me in particular, such a conclusion would be an evaluation not of the article itself, but only of its effect upon us.

Nor can we conclude that an article is poor because an author's thesis and interpretations are not convincing. White could have proved that smoke comes from smokestacks, but chose a more formidable task, to discover the underlying causes for our ecologic crisis. In evaluating a work, we must consider the aim of the author and his skill in striving to attain it. Lynn White has presented an ingenious and articulate argument offering us a unique perspective on our ecologic crisis. His work merits praise.

In a final evaluation of White's article we must, as from the beginning, strive to understand his point; did men under the influence of Christianity become indifferent to nature? Note the significant terms in the article: for example, pagans, spirits in nature, Christianity, doctrine of man's supremacy, indifference toward nature, marriage of science and technology. What do these terms mean? Did what White claims to have happened actually happen? Perhaps Lynn White has raised for some of us an important question.

The above discussion is the barest introduction to reading history. There are many types of books, and countless factors must be considered if we are to read intelligently. In general, however, reading is striving to understand what a person has done (or failed to do) with his material. Hence, in evaluating a work or in writing a review of a book or an article, do not merely summarize information; rather, identify and analyze what an author has done with his subject. In a book review, for example, you might, in the following order, identify the subject, scope, and aim of the book, state the argument and thesis, criticize them, and render your final evaluation of the work. And whether you praise or criticize an author's work, support your evaluation with specific examples. You might note that the author imaginatively located an obscure source, or that he failed to consult other sources vital for an understanding of his subject.

A conversation with Aldous Huxley not infrequently put one at the receiving end of an unforgettable monologue. About a year before his lamented death he was discoursing on a favorite topic: Man's unnatural treatment of nature and its sad results. To illustrate his point he told how, during the previous summer, he had returned to a little valley in England where he had spent many happy months as a child. Once it had been composed of delightful grassy glades; now it was becoming overgrown with unsightly brush because the rabbits that formerly kept such growth under control had largely succumbed to a disease, myxomatosis, that was deliberately introduced by the local farmers to reduce the rabbits' destruction of crops. Being something of a Philistine, I could be silent no longer, even in the interests of great rhetoric. I interrupted to point out that the rabbit itself had been brought as a domestic animal to England in 1176, presumably to improve the protein diet of the peasantry.

All forms of life modify their contexts. The most spectacular and benign instance is doubtless the coral polyp. By serving its own ends, it has created a vast undersea world favorable to thousands of other kinds of animals and plants. Ever since man became a numerous species he has affected his environment notably. The hypothesis that his fire-drive method of hunting created the world's great grasslands and helped to exterminate the monster mammals of the Pleistocene from much of the globe is plausible, if not proved. For 6 millennia at least, the banks of the lower Nile have been a human artifact rather than the swampy African jungle which nature, apart from man, would have made it. The Aswan Dam, flooding 5000 square miles, is only the latest stage in a long process. In many regions terracing or irrigation, overgrazing, the cutting of forests by Romans to build ships to fight Carthaginians or by Crusaders to solve the logistics problems of their expeditions, have profoundly changed some ecologies. Observation that the French landscape falls into two basic types, the open fields of the north and the *bocage* of the south and west, inspired Marc Bloch to undertake his classic study of medieval agricultural methods. Quite unintentionally, changes in human ways often affect nonhuman nature. It has been noted, for example, that the advent of the automobile eliminated huge flocks of sparrows that once fed on the horse manure littering every street.

The history of ecologic change is still so rudimentary that we know little about what really happened, or what the results were. The extinction of the European aurochs as late as 1627 would seem to have been a simple case of overenthusiastic hunting. On more intricate matters it often is impossible to find solid information. For a thousand years or more the Frisians and Hollanders have been pushing back the North Sea, and the process is culminating in our own time in the reclamation of the Zuider Zee. What, if any, species of animals, birds, fish, shore life, or plants have died out in the process? In their epic combat with Neptune have the Netherlanders overlooked ecological values in such a way that the quality of human life in the Netherlands has suffered? I cannot discover that the questions have ever been asked, much less answered.

People, then, have often been a dynamic element in their own environment, but in the present state of historical scholarship we usually do not know exactly when, where, or with what effects man-induced changes came. As we enter the last third of the 20th century, however, concern for the problem of ecologic backlash is mounting feverishly. Natural science, conceived as the effort to understand the nature of things, had flourished in several eras and among several peoples. Similarly there had been an age-old accumulation of technological skills, sometimes growing rapidly, sometimes slowly. But it was not until about four generations ago that Western Europe and North America arranged a marriage between science and technology, a union of the theoretical and the empirical approaches to our natural environment. The emergence in widespread practice of the Baconian creed that scientific knowledge means technological power over nature can scarcely be dated before about 1850, save in the chemical industries, where it is anticipated in the 18th century. Its acceptance as a normal pattern of action may mark the greatest event in human history since the invention of agriculture, and perhaps in nonhuman terrestrial history as well.

Almost at once the new situation forced the crystallization of the novel concept of ecology; indeed, the word *ecology* first appeared in the English language in 1873. Today, less than a century later, the impact of our race upon the environment has so increased in force that it has changed in essence. When the first cannons were fired, in the early 14th century, they affected ecology by sending workers scrambling to the forests and mountains for more potash, sulfur, iron ore, and charcoal, with some resulting erosion and deforestation. Hydrogen bombs are of a different order: a war fought with them might alter the genetics of all life on this planet. By 1285 London had a smog problem arising from the burning of soft coal, but our present combustion of fossil fuels threatens to change the chemistry of the globe's atmosphere as a whole, with consequences which we are only beginning to guess. With the population explosion, the carcinoma of planless urbanism, the new geological deposits of sewage and garbage, surely no creature other than man has ever managed to foul its nest in such short order.

There are many calls to action, but specific proposals, however worthy as individual items, seem too partial, palliative, negative: ban the bomb, tear down the billboards, give the Hindus contraceptives and tell them to eat their sacred cows. The simplest solution to any suspect change is, of course, to stop it, or, better yet, to revert to a romanticized past: make those ugly gasoline stations look like Anne Hathaway's cottage or (in the Far West) like ghost-town saloons. The "wilderness area" mentality invariably advocates deep-freezing an ecology, whether San Gimignano or the High Sierra, as it was before the first Kleenex was dropped. But neither atavism nor prettification will cope with the ecologic crisis of our time.

What shall we do? No one yet knows. Unless we think about fundamentals, our specific measures may produce new backlashes more serious than those they are designed to remedy.

As a beginning we should try to clarify our thinking by looking, in some historical depth, at the presuppositions that underlie modern technology and science. Science was traditionally aristocratic, speculative, intellectual in intent; technology was lower-class, empirical, action-oriented. The quite sudden fusion of these two, towards the middle of the 19th century, is surely related to the slightly prior and contemporary democratic revolutions which, by reducing social barriers, tended to assert a functional unity of brain and hand. Our ecologic crisis is the product of an emerging, entirely novel, democratic culture. The issue is whether a democratized world can survive its own implications. Presumably we cannot unless we rethink our axioms.

The Western Traditions of Technology and Science

One thing is so certain that it seems stupid to verbalize it: both modern technology and modern science are distinctively *Occidental*.

Our technology has absorbed elements from all over the world, notably from China; yet everywhere today, whether in Japan or in Nigeria, successful technology is Western. Our science is the heir to all the sciences of the past, especially perhaps to the work of the great Islamic scientists of the Middle Ages, who so often outdid the ancient Greeks in skill and perspicacity: al-Rāzī in medicine, for example; or ibn-al-Haytham in optics; or Omar Khayyám in mathematics. Indeed, not a few works of such geniuses seem to have vanished in the original Arabic and to survive only in medieval Latin translations that helped to lay the foundations for later Western developments. Today, around the globe, all significant science is Western in style and method, whatever the pigmentation or language of the scientists.

A second pair of facts is less well recognized because they result from quite recent historical scholarship. The leadership of the West, both in technology and in science, is far older than the so-called Scientific Revolution of the 17th century or the so-called Industrial Revolution of the 18th century. These terms are in fact outmoded and obscure the true nature of what they try to describe—significant stages in two long and separate developments. By A.D. 1000 at the latest—and perhaps, feebly, as much as 200 years earlier—the West began to apply water power to industrial processes other than milling grain. This was followed in the late 12th century by the harnessing of wind power. From simple beginnings, but with remarkable consistency of style, the West rapidly expanded its skills in the development of power machinery, labor-saving devices, and automation. Those who doubt should contemplate that most monumental achievement in the history of automation: the weight-driven mechanical clock, which appeared in two forms in the early 14th century. Not in craftsmanship but in basic technological capacity, the Latin West of the later Middle Ages far outstripped its elaborate, sophisticated, and esthetically magnificent sister cultures, Byzantium and Islam. In 1444 a great Greek ecclesiastic, Bessarion, who had gone to Italy, wrote a letter to a prince in Greece. He is amazed by the superiority of Western ships, arms, textiles, glass. But above all he is astonished by the spectacle of waterwheels sawing timbers and pumping the bellows of blast furnaces. Clearly, he had seen nothing of the sort in the Near East.

By the end of the 15th century the technological superiority of Europe was such that its small, mutually hostile nations could spill out over all the rest of the world, conquering, looting, and colonizing. The symbol of this technological superiority is the fact that Portugal, one of the weakest states of the Occident, was able to become, and to remain for a century, mistress of the East Indies. And we must remember that the technology of Vasco da Gama and Albuquerque was built by pure empiricism, drawing remarkably little support or inspiration from science.

In the present-day vernacular understanding, modern science is supposed to have begun in 1543, when both Copernicus and Vesalius published their great works. It is no derogation of their accomplishments, however, to point out that such structures as the *Fabrica* and the *De revolutionibus* do not appear overnight. The distinctive Western tradition of science, in fact, began in the late 11th century with a massive movement of translation of Arabic and Greek scientific works into Latin. A few notable books—Theophrastus, for example—escaped the West's avid new appetite for science, but within less than 200 years virtually the entire corpus of Greek and Muslim science was available in Latin and was being eagerly read and criticized in the new European universities. Out of criticism arose new observation, speculation, and increasing distrust of ancient authorities. By the late 13th century Europe had seized global scientific leadership from the faltering hands of Islam. It would be as absurd to deny the profound originality of Newton, Galileo, or Copernicus as to deny that of the 14th century scholastic scientists like Buridan or Oresme on whose work they built. Before the 11th century, science scarcely existed in the Latin West, even in Roman times. From the 11th century onward, the scientific sector of Occidental culture has increased in a steady crescendo.

Since both our technological and our scientific movements got their start, acquired their character, and achieved world dominance in the Middle Ages, it would seem that we cannot understand their nature or their present impact upon ecology without examining fundamental medieval assumptions and developments.

Medieval View of Man and Nature

Until recently, agriculture has been the chief occupation even in "advanced" societies; hence, any change in methods of tillage has much importance. Early plows, drawn by two oxen, did not normally turn the sod but merely scratched it. Thus, cross-plowing was needed and fields tended to be squarish. In the fairly light soils and semiarid climates of the Near East and Mediterranean, this worked well. But such a plow was inappropriate to the wet climate and often sticky soils of northern

Europe. By the latter part of the 7th century after Christ, however, following obscure beginnings, certain northern peasants were using an entirely new kind of plow, equipped with a vertical knife to cut the line of the furrow, a horizontal share to slice under the sod, and a moldboard to turn it over. The friction of this plow with the soil was so great that it normally required not two but eight oxen. It attacked the land with such violence that cross-plowing was not needed, and fields tended to be shaped in long strips.

In the days of the scratch-plow, fields were distributed generally in units capable of supporting a single family. Subsistence farming was the presupposition. But no peasant owned eight oxen: to use the new and more efficient plow, peasants pooled their oxen to form large plow-teams, originally receiving (it would appear) plowed strips in proportion to their contribution. Thus, distribution of land was based no longer on the needs of a family but, rather, on the capacity of a power machine to till the earth. Man's relation to the soil was profoundly changed. Formerly man had been part of nature; now he was the exploiter of nature. Nowhere else in the world did farmers develop any analogous agricultural implement. Is it coincidence that modern technology, with its ruthlessness toward nature, has so largely been produced by descendants of these peasants of northern Europe?

This same exploitive attitude appears slightly before A.D. 830 in Western illustrated calendars. In older calendars the months were shown as passive personifications. The new Frankish calendars, which set the style for the Middle Ages, are very different: they show men coercing the world around them—plowing, harvesting, chopping trees, butchering pigs. Man and nature are two things, and man is master.

These novelties seem to be in harmony with larger intellectual patterns. What people do about their ecology depends on what they think about themselves in relation to things around them. Human ecology is deeply conditioned by beliefs about our nature and destiny—that is, by religion. To Western eyes this is very evident in, say, India or Ceylon. It is equally true of ourselves and of our medieval ancestors.

The victory of Christianity over paganism was the greatest psychic revolution in the history of our culture. It has become fashionable today to say that, for better or worse, we live in "the post-Christian age." Certainly the forms of our thinking and language have largely ceased to be Christian, but to my eye the substance often remains amazingly akin to that of the past. Our daily habits of action, for example, are dominated by an implicit faith in perpetual progress which was unknown either to Greco-Roman antiquity or to the Orient. It is rooted in, and is indefensible apart from, Judeo-Christian teleology. The fact that Communists share it merely helps to show what can be demonstrated on many other grounds: that Marxism, like Islam, is a Judeo-Christian heresy. We continue today to live, as we have lived for about 1700 years, very largely in a context of Christian axioms.

What did Christianity tell people about their relations with the environment?

While many of the world's mythologies provide stories of creation, Greco-Roman mythology was singularly incoherent in this respect. Like Aristotle, the intellectuals of the ancient West denied that the visible world had had a beginning. Indeed, the idea of a beginning was impossible in the framework of their cyclical notion of time. In sharp contrast, Christianity inherited from Judaism not only a concept of time as nonrepetitive and linear but also a striking story of creation. By gradual stages a loving and all-powerful God had created light and darkness, the heavenly bodies, the earth and all its plants, animals, birds, and fishes. Finally, God had created Adam and, as an after-thought, Eve to keep man from being lonely. Man named all the animals, thus establishing his dominance over them. God planned all of this explicitly for man's benefit and rule: no item in the physical creation had any purpose save to serve man's purposes. And, although man's body is made of clay, he is not simply part of nature: he is made in God's image.

Especially in its Western form, Christianity is the most anthropocentric religion the world has seen. As early as the 2nd century both Tertullian and Saint Irenaeus of Lyons were insisting that when God shaped Adam he was foreshadowing the image of the incarnate Christ, the Second Adam. Man shares, in great measure, God's transcendence of nature. Christianity, in absolute contrast to ancient paganism and Asia's religions (except, perhaps, Zoroastrianism), not only established a dualism of man and nature but also insisted that it is God's will that man exploit nature for his proper ends.

At the level of the common people this worked out in an interesting way. In Antiquity every tree, every spring, every stream, every hill had its own *genius loci*, its guardian spirit. These spirits were accessible to men, but were very unlike men; centaurs, fauns, and mermaids show their ambivalence. Before one cut a tree, mined a mountain, or dammed a brook, it was important to placate the spirit in charge of that particular situation, and to keep it placated. By destroying pagan animism, Christianity made it possible to exploit nature in a mood of indifference to the feelings of natural objects.

It is often said that for animism the Church substituted the cult of saints. True; but the cult of saints is functionally quite different from animism. The saint is not *in* natural objects; he may have special shrines, but his citizenship is in heaven. Moreover, a saint is entirely a man; he can be approached in human terms. In addition to saints, Christianity of course also had angels and demons inherited from Judaism and perhaps, at one remove, from Zoroastrianism. But these were all as mobile as the saints themselves. The spirits *in* natural objects, which formerly had protected nature from man, evaporated. Man's effective monopoly on spirit in this world was confirmed, and the old inhibitions to the exploitation of nature crumbled.

When one speaks in such sweeping terms, a note of caution is in order. Christianity is a complex faith, and its consequences differ in differing contexts. What I have said may well apply to the medieval West, where in fact technology made spectacular advances. But the Greek East, a highly civilized realm of equal Christian devotion, seems to have produced no marked technological innovation after the late 7th century, when Greek fire was invented. The key to the contrast may perhaps be found in a difference in the tonality of piety and thought which students of comparative theology find between the Greek and the Latin Churches. The Greeks believed that sin was intellectual blindness, and that salvation was found in illumination, orthodoxy—that is, clear thinking. The Latins, on the other hand, felt that sin was moral evil, and that salvation was to be found in right conduct. Eastern theology has been intellectualist. Western theology has been voluntarist. The Greek saint contemplates; the Western saint acts. The implications of Christianity for the conquest of nature would emerge more easily in the Western atmosphere.

The Christian dogma of creation, which is found in the first clause of all the Creeds, has another meaning for our comprehension of today's ecologic crisis. By revelation, God had given man the Bible, the Book of Scripture. But since God had made nature, nature also must reveal the divine mentality. The religious study of nature for the better understanding of God was known as natural theology. In the early Church, and always in the Greek East, nature was conceived primarily as a symbolic system through which God speaks to men: the ant is a sermon to sluggards; rising flames are the symbol of the soul's aspiration. This view of nature was essentially artistic rather than scientific. While Byzantium preserved and copied great numbers of ancient Greek scientific texts, science as we conceive it could scarcely flourish in such an ambience.

However, in the Latin West by the early 13th century natural theology was following a very different bent. It was ceasing to be the decoding of the physical symbols of God's communication with man and was becoming the effort to understand God's mind by discovering how his creation operates. The rainbow was no longer simply a symbol of hope first sent to Noah after the Deluge: Robert Grosseteste, Friar Roger Bacon, and Theodoric of Freiberg produced startlingly sophisticated work on the optics of the rainbow, but they did it as a venture in religious understanding. From the 13th century onward, up to and including Leibnitz and Newton, every major scientist, in effect, explained his motivations in religious terms. Indeed, if Galileo had not been so expert an amateur theologian he would have got into far less trouble: the professionals resented his intrusion. And Newton seems to have regarded himself more as a theologian than as a scientist. It was not until the late 18th century that the hypothesis of God became unnecessary to many scientists.

It is often hard for the historian to judge, when men explain why they are doing what they want to do, whether they are offering real reasons or merely culturally acceptable reasons. The consistency with which scientists during the long formative centuries of Western science said that the task and the reward of the scientist was "to think God's thoughts after him" leads one to believe that this was their real motivation. If so, then modern Western science was cast in a matrix of Christian theology. The dynamism of religious devotion, shaped by the Judeo-Christian dogma of creation, gave it impetus.

An Alternative Christian View

We would seem to be headed toward conclusions unpalatable to many Christians. Since both *science* and *technology* are blessed words in our contemporary vocabulary, some may be happy at the notions, first, that, viewed historically, modern science is an extrapolation of natural theology and, second, that modern technology is at least partly to be explained as an Occidental, voluntarist realization of the Christian dogma of man's transcendence of, and rightful mastery over, nature. But, as we now recognize, somewhat over a century ago science and technology—hitherto quite separate activities—joined to give mankind powers which, to judge by many of the ecologic effects, are out of control. If so, Christianity bears a huge burden of guilt.

I personally doubt that disastrous ecologic backlash can be avoided simply by applying to our problems more science and more technology. Our science and technology have grown out of Christian attitudes toward man's relation to nature which are almost universally held not only by Christians and neo-Christians but also by those who fondly regard themselves as post-Christians. Despite Copernicus, all the cosmos rotates around our little globe. Despite Darwin, we are *not*, in our hearts, part of the natural process. We are superior to nature, contemptuous of it, willing to use it for our slightest whim. The newly elected Governor of California, like myself a churchman but less troubled than I, spoke for the Christian tradition when he said (as is alleged), "when you've seen one redwood tree, you've seen them all." To a Christian a tree can be no more than a physical fact. The whole concept of the sacred grove is alien to Christianity and to the ethos of the West. For nearly 2 millennia Christian missionaries have been chopping down sacred groves, which are idolatrous because they assume spirit in nature.

What we do about ecology depends on our ideas of the man-nature relationship. More science and more technology are not going to get us out of the present ecologic crisis until we find a new religion, or rethink our old one. The beatniks, who are the basic revolutionaries of our time, show a sound instinct in their affinity for Zen Buddhism, which conceives of the man-nature relationship as very nearly the mirror image of the Christian view. Zen, however, is as deeply conditioned by Asian history as Christianity is by the experience of the West, and I am dubious of its viability among us.

Possibly we should ponder the greatest radical in Christian history since Christ: Saint Francis of Assisi. The prime miracle of Saint Francis is the fact that he did not end at the stake, as many of his left-wing followers did. He was so clearly heretical that a General of the Franciscan Order, Saint Bonaventura, a great and perceptive Christian, tried to suppress the early accounts of Franciscanism. The key to an understanding of Francis is his belief in the virtue of humility—not merely for the individual but for man as a species. Francis tried to depose man from his monarchy over creation and set up a democracy of all God's creatures. With him the ant is no longer simply a homily for the lazy, flames a sign of the thrust of the soul toward union with God;

now they are Brother Ant and Sister Fire, praising the Creator in their own ways as Brother Man does in his.

Later commentators have said that Francis preached to the birds as a rebuke to men who would not listen. The records do not read so: he urged the little birds to praise God, and in spiritual ecstasy they flapped their wings and chirped rejoicing. Legends of saints, especially the Irish saints, had long told of their dealings with animals but always, I believe, to show their human dominance over creatures. With Francis it is different. The land around Gubbio in the Apennines was being ravaged by a fierce wolf. Saint Francis, says the legend, talked to the wolf and persuaded him of the error of his ways. The wolf repented, died in the odor of sanctity, and was buried in consecrated ground.

What Sir Steven Ruciman calls "the Franciscan doctrine of the animal soul" was quickly stamped out. Quite possibly it was in part inspired, consciously or unconsciously, by the belief in reincarnation held by the Cathar heretics who at that time teemed in Italy and southern France, and who presumably had got it originally from India. It is significant that at just the same moment, about 1200, traces of metempsychosis are found also in western Judaism, in the Provençal *Cabbala*. But Francis held neither to transmigration of souls nor to pantheism. His view of nature and of man rested on a unique sort of pan-psychism of all things animate and inanimate, designed for the glorification of their transcendent Creator, who, in the ultimate gesture of cosmic humility, assumed flesh, lay helpless in a manger, and hung dying on a scaffold.

I am not suggesting that many contemporary Americans who are concerned about our ecologic crisis will be either able or willing to counsel with wolves or exhort birds. However, the present increasing disruption of the global environment is the product of a dynamic technology and science which were originating in the Western medieval world against which Saint Francis was rebelling in so original a way. Their growth cannot be understood historically apart from distinctive attitudes toward nature which are deeply grounded in Christian dogma. The fact that most people do not think of these attitudes as Christian is irrelevant. No new set of basic values has been accepted in our society to displace those of Christianity. Hence we shall continue to have a worsening ecologic crisis until we reject the Christian axiom that nature has no reason for existence save to serve man.

The greatest spiritual revolutionary in Western history, Saint Francis, proposed what he thought was an alternative Christian view of nature and man's relation to it: he tried to substitute the idea of the equality of all creatures, including man, for the idea of man's limitless rule of creation. He failed. Both our present science and our present technology are so tinctured with orthodox Christian arrogance toward nature that no solution for our ecologic crisis can be expected from them alone. Since the roots of our trouble are so largely religious, the remedy must also be essentially religious, whether we call it that or not. We must rethink and refeel our nature and destiny. The profoundly religious, but heretical, sense of the primitive Franciscans for the spiritual autonomy of all parts of nature may point a direction. I propose Francis as a patron saint for ecologists.

Appendix III: **Outline of the Dewey Decimal Classification**

Reproduced in this appendix is an outline of the Dewey Decimal Classification (Second Summary: The 100 Divisions, with excerpts from the Third Summary: The 1000 Divisions).[1] On the use of this outline, see Chapter Three, pp. 27–33. The numbers in the outline (e.g. 100, 200) are the library call numbers identifying books in libraries using the Dewey Decimal Classification (see Appendix IV for the Library of Congress Classification).

000	Generalities
010	Bibliographies & catalogs
020	Library & information sciences
030	General encyclopedic works
050	General serial publications
060	General organizations & museology
070	Journalism, publishing, newspapers
080	General collections
090	Manuscripts & book rarities
100	Philosophy & related disciplines
108	Collections of philosophy
109	Historical treatment of philosophy
110	Metaphysics
120	Knowledge, cause, purpose, man
130	Popular & parapsychology, occultism
140	Specific philosophical viewpoints
150	Psychology
160	Logic
170	Ethics (Moral philosophy)
180	Ancient, medieval, Oriental

1. Reproduced from the Edition 18 *DEWEY Decimal Classification* by permission of Forest Press, Inc., owner of copyright (*DEWEY Decimal Classification and Relative Index*, devised by Melvil Dewey, edition 18, 3 vols., Forest Press, Inc., 1971).

190 Modern Western philosophy
200 Religion
  208 Collections of Christianity
  209 History & geography of Christianity
210 Natural religion
220 Bible
230 Christian doctrinal theology
240 Christian moral & devotional
250 Local church & religious orders
260 Social & ecclesiastical theology
270 History & geography of church
  271 Religious congregations & orders
  272 Persecutions
  273 Doctrinal controversies & heresies
  274 Christian church in Europe
  275 Christian church in Asia
  276 Christian church in Africa
  277 Christian church in North America
  278 Christian church in South America
  279 Christian church in other areas
280 Christian denominations & sects
290 Other religions & comparative
300 The social sciences
310 Statistics
320 Political science
  321 Forms of states
  322 Relation of state to social groups
  323 Relation of state to its residents
  324 Electoral process
  325 International migration
  326 Slavery & emancipation
  327 International relations
  328 Legislation
  329 Practical politics

330   Economics
340   Law
    341   International law
    342   Constitutional & administrative law
    343   Miscellaneous public law
    344   Social law
    345   Criminal law
    346   Private law
    347   Civil procedure
    348   Statutes, regulations, cases
350   Public administration
360   Social pathology & services
370   Education
380   Commerce
390   Customs & folklore
    391   Costume & personal appearance
    392   Customs of life cycle & domestic life
    393   Death customs
    394   General customs
    395   Etiquette
    398   Folklore
    399   Customs of war & diplomacy
400   Language
410   Linguistics
420   English & Anglo-Saxon languages
430   Germanic languages   German
440   Romance languages   French
450   Italian, Romanian, Rhaeto-Romanic
460   Spanish & Portuguese languages
470   Italic languages   Latin
480   Hellenic   Classical Greek
490   Other languages
500   Pure sciences
    508   Collections, travels, surveys

509 Historical & geographical treatment
510 Mathematics
520 Astronomy & allied sciences
530 Physics
540 Chemistry & allied sciences
550 Sciences of earth & other worlds
560 Paleontology
570 Life sciences
580 Botanical sciences
590 Zoological sciences
600 Technology (Applied sciences)
609 Historical & geographical treatment
610 Medical sciences
620 Engineering & allied operations
630 Agriculture & related
640 Domestic arts & sciences
650 Managerial services
660 Chemical & related technologies
670 Manufactures
680 Miscellaneous manufactures
690 Buildings
700 The arts
709 Historical & geographical treatment
710 Civic & landscape art
720 Architecture
 721 Architectural construction
 722 Ancient & Oriental architecture
 723 Medieval architecture
 724 Modern architecture
 725 Public structures
 726 Buildings for religious purposes
 727 Buildings for educational purposes
 728 Residential buildings
 729 Design & decoration

932   Egypt
933   Palestine
934   India
935   Mesopotamia & Iranian Plateau
936   Northern & western Europe
937   Italian peninsula & adjacent areas
938   Greece
939   Other parts of ancient world
940   General history of Europe
941   Scotland & Ireland
942   British Isles   England
943   Central Europe   Germany
944   France
945   Italy
946   Iberian Peninsula   Spain
947   Eastern Europe   Soviet Union
948   Northern Europe   Scandinavia
949   Other parts of Europe
950   General history of Asia
951   China & adjacent areas
952   Japan & adjacent islands
953   Arabian Peninsula & adjacent areas
954   South Asia   India
955   Iran (Persia)
956   Middle East (Near East)
957   Siberia (Asiatic Russia)
958   Central Asia
959   Southeast Asia
960   General history of Africa
961   North Africa
962   Countries of the Nile   Egypt
963   Ethiopia (Abyssinia)
964   Northwest coast & offshore islands
965   Algeria

Appendix IV: Outline of the Library of Congress Classification System

On the use of this outline of the Library of Congress Classification (abridged from the 2nd edition issued in Washington, D.C., 1970), see Chapter Three, pages 27–33. The letters (A, BR, etc.) and numbers (10–41, 5–100) are the call numbers by which books are arranged on the library shelves. I have noted with asterisks (*) those sections of the library most likely to yield historical information (as opposed to technical and contemporary material).

MAJOR CLASSIFICATIONS

A General works

B Philosophy. Psychology. Religion*

C Auxiliary sciences of History*

D History: general and Old World*

E–F History: America*

G Geography. Anthropology. Recreation*

H Social Sciences*

J Political Science*

K Law

L Education

M Music

N Fine Arts*

P Language and Literature

Q Science

R Medicine

S Agriculture

T Technology

U Military science

V Naval science

Z Bibliography and Library Science

A. GENERAL WORKS. POLYGRAPHY

AC Collections. Series. Collected works. Collections of monographs, essays, etc. (1–195)

AE Encyclopedias (General)

AG Dictionaries and other general reference works. Dictionaries. Minor encyclopedias (1–91)—including popular and juvenile encyclopedias

AI Indexes (General)

AM Museums (General). Collectors and collecting (General)

AN Newspapers—For history and description of individual newspapers, *see* PN4891–5650

AP Periodicals (General)
Humorous (101–115); Juvenile (200–230)

AS Academies and learned societies (General)
International associations, congresses, etc. (3–4)

AY Yearbooks. Almanacs. Directories—For general works only Almanacs (30–1725); Directories (2001)—For general works on theory, methods of compilation, etc.

AZ History of the sciences in general. Scholarship and learning
Popular errors, delusions and superstitions (999)

B. *PHILOSOPHY. PSYCHOLOGY. RELIGION (Many sections may be useful to the history student)

B Philosophy (General)
*History and systems (69–5739)—including individual philosophers and schools of philosophy

BC Logic

BD Speculative philosophy
General philosophical works (10–41); Metaphysics (95–131); Epistemology. Theory of knowledge (143–236); Methodology (240–241); Ontology (300–450); Cosmology (493–708)

BF Psychology
Sensation (231–299); Cognition. Perception. Intelligence (311–499); Emotion (511–593); Will (608–635); Applied psychology (636–637); Comparative psychology (660–687); Personality (698); Genetic psychology. Child psychology (699–755); Temperament. Character (795–839); Physiognomy (840–861); Phrenology (866–885); Graphology (889–905); The hand. Palmistry (908–940)
Parapsychology (1001–1389)—including hallucinations, sleep, dreams, hypnotism, etc.
Occult sciences (1405–1999)—including ghosts, demonology, witchcraft, astrology, oracles, fortunetelling

BH Aesthetics

BJ Ethics

Practical and applied ethics. Conduct of life (1545–1725)
Social usages. Etiquette (1801–2195)

Religion

BL Religions. Mythology. Rationalism.
Natural theology (175–290); Mythology (General) (300–325);
Religious doctrines (General) (425–490); Eschatology
(500–547); Worship. Cultus (550–619)
History and principles of particular religions (660–2670)—including Brahmanism, Hinduism, Buddhism
Rationalism (2700–2790)

BM Judaism

BP Islam. Bahaism. Theosophy, etc.

Christianity

BR *Christianity (General)
Collections (45–85)—including early Christian literature
Church history (140–1500)
Biography (1690–1725)

BS The Bible and exegesis

BT Doctrinal theology. Apologetics

BV Practical theology
Worship (5–525)—including the church year, Christian symbols, liturgy, prayer, hymnology
Ecclesiastical theology (590–1650)—including the Church, church and state, church management, ministry, sacraments, religious societies, religious education
Missions (2000–3705); Evangelism. Revivals (3750–3799); Pastoral theology (4000–4470); Practical religion. The Christian life (4485–5099)

BX Denominations and sects
Church unity. Ecumenical movement (1–9)
Eastern churches. Oriental churches (100–750)
Roman Catholic Church (800–4795)
Protestantism (4800–9999)

C. *AUXILIARY SCIENCES OF HISTORY (All sections useful to the history student)

C   Auxiliary sciences of history (General)

CB   History of civilization and culture (General)

CC   Archaeology (General)
     Bells. Campanology (200–260); Crosses (300–350)

CD   Diplomatics. Archives. Seals: Archives (931–4279)

CE   Technical chronology. Calendar—For historical chronology, *see* D–F

CJ   Numismatics—including Tokens (4801–5450); Medals, etc. (5501–6651)

CN   Epigraphy. Inscriptions

CR   Heraldry
     Crests, monograms, etc. (51–93); Flags, banners, and standards (101–115); Public and official heraldry (191–1020); Ecclesiastical and sacred heraldry (1101–1131); Family heraldry (1179–3400); Titles of honor, etc. (3499–4420); Chivalry and knighthood (4501–6305)

CS   Genealogy—including Personal and family names (2300–3090)

CT   Biography
     Collections (General. Universal) (93–206)
     National biography (210–3150)
     Biography of women (3200–3830)

D. *HISTORY: GENERAL AND OLD WORLD—including geography and description of individual regions and countries (All sections useful to the history student)

D   History (General)
     Ancient history (51–95)
     Medieval history (111–203)
     Modern history (204–849)
       World War I (501–680)
       World War II (731–838)
     Europe (General) (901–1075)

DA   Great Britain
     Ireland (900–995)

DB   Austria. Czechoslovakia. Hungary

DC   France

DD   Germany

DE   The Mediterranean region. Greco-Roman world

DF   Greece

DG   Italy

DH–DJ Belgium. Holland. Luxembourg

DK   Russia—including Poland (401–443); Finland (445–465)

DL   Northern Europe. Scandinavia

DP   Spain. Portugal

DQ   Switzerland

DR   Eastern Europe. Balkan Peninsula. Turkey

DS   Asia

DT   Africa

DU   Oceania (South Seas)—including Australia (80–398); New Zealand (400–430)

DX   Gypsies

E–F.   *HISTORY: AMERICA (All sections useful to the history student)

E   America (General) (11–29)
          North America (31–45)
          Indians. Indians of North America (51–99)
          Discovery of America and early explorations (101–135)

United States (General)

          Elements in the population (184–185)—including Negroes (185)
          Colonial history (186–199)
          Revolution (201–298)
          Revolution to the Civil War (301–453)
             War of 1812 (351–364)
             War with Mexico (401–415)
             Slavery (441–453)
          Civil War (456–655)
             Confederate States of America (482–489)
          Late nineteenth century (660–738)

Spanish-American War (714–735)
Twentieth century (740–   )

F United States local history (1–975)
British America. Canada (1001–1140)
Mexico (1201–1392)
Latin America (General) (1401–1419)
Central America (1421–1577)
West Indies (1601–2175)
South America (General) (2201–2239)
Colombia (2251–2299); Venezuela (2301–2349)
Guiana (2351–2471); Brazil (2501–2659)
Paraguay (2661–2699); Uruguay (2701–2799)
Argentina (2801–3021); Chile (3051–3285)
Bolivia (3301–3359); Peru (3401–3619)
Ecuador (3701–3799)

G. *GEOGRAPHY. ANTHROPOLOGY. RECREATION
(Many sections useful to the history student)

G Geography (General)
Voyages and travels (General) (149–570)—including discoveries, explorations, mountaineering, etc.
Polar regions (575–890)—including exploration, history, description
Atlases (1001–3102); Maps (3160–9980)

GA Mathematical geography. Cartography
Mathematical geography (1–87); Cartography (101–1999)

GB Physical geography—including arrangement by country
Geomorphology (401–648); Water. Hydrology (651–2598)

GC Oceanography
Seawater (101–181); Dynamics of the sea (201–376); Marine sediments (380–399); Marine resources (1015–1023); Marine pollution (1080–1572)

GF Anthropogeography. Human ecology

GN Anthropology
Physical anthropology. Somatology (51–211)
Physiological and psychological anthropology (221–279)
Ethnology and ethnography (307–686)—including primitive

customs and institutions, individual races and ethnic groups

Prehistoric archaeology (700–875)—including arrangement by country

GR *Folklore—including Folklore relating to special subjects (440–950)

GT *Manners and customs (General)

Houses. Dwellings (170–482)

Dress. Costume. Fashion (500–2370)

Customs relative to private and public life (2400–5090)—including love, marriage, eating, smoking, treatment of the dead, town life, customs of chivalry, festivals and holidays

Customs relative to special classes, by birth, occupation, etc. (5320–6715)

GV Recreation

Organized camping. Summer camps (192–198); Physical training (201–547); Sports (561–1197); Games and amusements (1200–1570); Dancing (1580–1799); Circuses, carnivals, etc. (1800–1860)

H. *SOCIAL SCIENCES (Many sections useful to the history student)

H Social sciences (General)

HA Statistics—including collections of general and census statistics of special countries. For mathematical statistics, *see* QA276 –279

Economics

HB Economic theory

Population (848–875)

Demography. Vital statistics (879–3700)

Crises. Business cycles (3711–3840)

HC *Economic history and conditions: National production

HD Land. Agriculture. Industry

Production. Industrial management (1–91)

Land (101–1395)—including public lands, real estate, land tenure

Agricultural economics (1401–2210)—including agricultural laborers

Industry (2321–9999)

Corporations. Trusts. Cartels (2709–2930); Industrial cooperation (2951–3570); The state and industrial organization (3611–4730)—including state industries, public works, municipal industries

Labor (4801–8942)—including wages, strikes, unemployment, labor unions, industrial relations, social security, professions, state labor. For civil service, *see* J Special industries and trades (9000–9999)

HE Transportation and communication

Traffic engineering. Roads and highways (331–377); Water transportation (381–971); Rail transportation (1001–5600); Automotive transportation (5601–5720); Postal service. Stamp collecting (6000–7500); Telecommunication. Telegraph (7601–8688); Radio and television (8689–8700); Telephone (8701–9715); Air transportation (9761–9900)

HF Commerce

Boards of trade. Chambers of commerce (294–343); Tariff policy (1701–2701); Business. Business administration (5001–5780)—including Personnel management (5549) and Accounting (5601–5689); Advertising (5801–6191)

HG Finance

Money (201–1492); Banking (1501–3542); Credit (3701–3781); Foreign exchange (3810–4000); Corporation finance (4001–4495); Stocks, investment, speculation (4501–6270); Insurance (8011–9970)

HJ Public finance

Income and expenditure. The budget (2005–2199); Revenue. Taxation (2240–5957); Customs. Tariff (6041–7384); Public credit. Debts. Loans (8003–8963); Local finance (9000–9698); Public accounting (9701–9995)

Sociology

HM Sociology (General and theoretical)—including Social Psychology (251–291)

HN *Social history. Social problems. Social reform. The church and
social problems (30–39)
Social groups

HQ The family. Marriage. Woman
Sexual life (12–449)
Erotica (450–471)
The family. Marriage (503–1064)—including child study, divorce, the aged, etc.
Woman. Feminism. Women's clubs (1101–2030)

HS Societies: Secret, benevolent, etc. Clubs—including Freemasons,
religious societies, ethnic societies, political societies, Boy
Scouts

HT Communities. Classes. Races
Urban sociology. Cities and towns (101–348)
Regional planning (390–395)
Rural sociology (401–485)
Social classes (601–1445)—including middle class, serfdom,
slavery
Races (1501–1595)

HV Social pathology. Social and public welfare. Criminology
Charities (40–696)
Protection, assistance and relief (697–4959)—including protection of animals
Alcoholism. Intemperance. Temperance reform (5001–5720);
Tobacco habit (5725–5770); Drug habits. Drug abuse
(5800–5840); Criminology (6001–9920)—including
crimes (6251–7220) and penology—prisons, police,
etc. (7231–9920)

HX Socialism. Communism. Anarchism—including Utopias (806–
811)

J. *POLITICAL SCIENCE (Many sections useful to the history
student)

J Official documents (General serial documents only)
Official gazettes (1–9)
United States documents. For congressional hearings, reports,
etc., *see* KF

Presidents' messages and other executive documents (80–85)

State documents (86–87)

Other countries (100–981). For documents issued by local governments, *see* JS

JA *Collections and general works

JC *Political theory. Theory of the state

Nationalism. Minorities. Geopolitics (311–323)

Nature, entity, concept of the state (325–341)

Symbolism, emblems of the state: Arms, flag, etc. (345–347)

Forms of the state (348–497)—including imperialism, the world state, monarchy, aristocracy, democracy, fascism, dictatorships

Purpose, functions, and relations of the state (501–628)

The state and the individual. Individual rights. Liberty (571–628)

Constitutional history and administration

JF General works. Comparative works

Organs and function of government (201–723)

Political rights and guaranties (800–1191)—including citizenship, suffrage, electoral systems, representation, the ballot

Government. Administration (1321–2112); Civil service (1411–1674); Political parties (2011–2112)

Special countries

JK United States

JL British America. Latin America

JN Europe

JQ Asia. Africa. Australia. Oceania

JS Local government

Serial documents (General) (3–37); Municipal government (141–231)

Local government other than municipal (241–285)

JV Colonies and colonization. Emigration and immigration

JX International law. International relations

Collections. Documents. Cases (63–1195)

Diplomatic relations (Universal collections) (101–115)

Treaties (Universal collections) (120–191)
International relations. Foreign relations (1305–1589)
Diplomacy. The diplomatic service (1625–1896)
International arbitration. World peace. International organiza-
tion (1901–1995)—including peace movements, Lea-
gue of Nations, United Nations, arbitration treaties,
international courts
International law (Treatises and monographs) (2001–5810)

K. LAW (Some sections useful to the history student)

K   *History of Law. Etc.

Law of the United States

KF   Federal law. Common and collective state law

KFA-

KFW Law of individual states, e.g. Alabama (KFA 0–599), Alaska
(KFA 1200–1799), Washington (KFW 0–599)

KFX Law of individual cities, A–Z

KFZ Law of individual territories

L. EDUCATION (Some sections useful to the history student)

L   Education (General)—For periodicals, congresses, directories,
etc.

LA   *History of education

LB   Theory and practice of education

LC   Special aspects of education
Forms of education (8–63)—including self, home, and private
school education
Social aspects of education (65–245)—including education and
the state, religious instruction in public schools, com-
pulsory education, illiteracy, educational sociology,
community and the school, endowments
Moral and religious education (251–951)
Types of education (1001–1091)—including humanistic, voca-
tional, and professional education
Education of special classes of persons (1390–5153)—including

women, Negroes, gifted and handicapped children, orphans, middle class

Adult education. Education extension (5201–6691)

Individual institutions: universities, colleges, and schools

LD   United States

LE   America, except United States

LF   Europe

LG   Asia. Africa. Oceania

LH   College and school magazines and papers

LJ   Student fraternities and societies, United States

LT   Textbooks—For textbooks covering several subjects. For textbooks on particular subjects, *see* those subjects in B–Z

M. MUSIC AND BOOKS ON MUSIC (A few sections useful to the history student)

M   Music

Instrumental music (5–1459)

Vocal music (1495–2199)—including National music (1627–1853)—including primitive, folk, traditional, patriotic, political, and typical music

Sacred vocal music (1999–2199)

ML Literature of music

Librettos (Texts for music) (48–54); Bibliography (111–157)

History and criticism (159–3795)—including biographies of composers

Instruments and instrumental music (460–1354)—including Chamber and orchestral music. Band (Military) (1100–1354)

Vocal music (1400–3275)—including Choral music (Sacred and secular) (1500–1554); Secular vocal music (1600–2862)—including dramatic music, cantatas, songs; Sacred vocal music (2900–3197)—including church music, oratorios

Dance music (3400–3465); National music (3545–3776)

Philosophy and physics of music (3800–3923)—including color and music, physiology, psychology, aesthetics, etc.

Fiction. Juvenile literature (3925–3930)

MT Music instruction and study

N. *FINE ARTS (Many sections useful to the history student)

N Visual arts (General)
Art museums, galleries, etc. (400–4040)—Arranged by country, subarrangement by city
Exhibitions (4390–5098)
Private collections and collectors (5200–5299)
History of art (5300–7418)
Technique, composition, style, etc. (7430–7433)
Art criticism (7475–7483)
Portraits (7575–7624)
Religious art (7790–8199)
Examination and conservation of works of art (8555–8580)
Economics of art (8600–8675)
Art and the state. Public art (8700–9165)

NA Architecture
History. Historical monuments (200–1613)
Architectural design and drawing (2700–2790)
Architectural details, motives, decoration, etc. (2835–4050)
Special classes of buildings (4100–8480)
Aesthetics of cities. City planning and beautification (9000–9425)

NB Sculpture

NC Drawing. Design. Illustration
Commercial art. Advertising art (997–1003); Caricature. Pictorial humor and satire (1300–1766); Posters (1800–1855)

ND Painting
Special subjects (1290–1460)—including human figure, landscapes, animals, still life, flowers
Watercolor painting (1700–2495); Mural painting (2550–2888)
Illuminating of manuscripts and books (2890–3416)

NE Print media
Printmaking and engraving (1–978)
Wood engraving. Woodcuts. Xylography (1000–1352)
Metal engraving. Copper, steel, etc. (1400–1879)—including color prints; Etching and aquatint (1940–2230); Serig-

raphy (2236–2239); Lithography (2250–2570); Printing of engravings (2800–2890)

NK Decorative arts. Applied arts. Decoration and ornament
Arts and crafts movement (1135–1149)
Interior decoration. House decoration (1700–3505)
Other arts and art industries (3600–9955)
  Ceramics. Pottery. Porcelain (3700–4695); Costume and its accessories (4700–4890); Enamel. Glass. Glyptic arts (5000–5735); Ivory carving. Ivories (5800–5998); Metalwork (6400–8459)—including armor, jewelry, plate, brasses, pewter; Textile arts and art needlework (8800–9505); Woodwork (9600–9955)—including carvings, fretwork, inlaying

NX Arts in general
Religious arts (654–694); Patronage of the arts (700–750); Special arts centers (800–820)

P. *LANGUAGE AND LITERATURE (Many sections useful to the history student—literature more than language)

P Philology and linguistics (General)
Communication. Mass media (87–96)
Language (General) (101–409)
  Philosophy, psychology, origin, etc. of language (101–112)
  Science of language. Linguistics (121–141)
  Comparative grammar (201–297); Style. Composition. Rhetoric (301); Translating and interpreting (306–310); Prosody. Metrics. Rhythmics (311); Lexicography (327–361); Linguistic geography (375–381)
Indo-European philology (501–769)
Extinct (Ancient or Medieval) Asiatic and European languages (901–1081)

PA Classical languages and literatures
Greek philology and language (227–1179)
Latin philology and language (2001–2915)
Greek literature
  Ancient (Classic) to ca. 600 A.D. (3051–4500)
  Byzantine and modern (5000–5665)
Latin literature
  Ancient Roman (6001–6971)

Medieval and modern (8001–8595)

Modern European languages

PB   General works (1–431)
Celtic languages and literatures
     Irish (1201–1449); Gaelic. Scottish Gaelic (1501–1709); Manx
        (1801–1888); Brythonic group (2001–3029)—including
        Welsh, Cornish, Breton, Gallic

PC   Romance languages
Romanian language and literature (601–872); Italian (1001–
        1977); French. Provençal (2001–3761); Catalan lan-
        guage and literature (3801–3976); Spanish (4001–
        4977); Portuguese (5001–5498)

PD   Germanic languages
Old Germanic dialects (1001–1350)—including Gothic, Van-
        dal, Burgundian, Langobardian
Scandinavian. North Germanic (1501–5929) Old Norse. Old
        Icelandic and Norwegian (2201–2392); Icelandic
        (2401–2489); Norwegian (2571–2999); Danish (3001–
        3929); Swedish (5001–5929)

PE   English

PF   West Germanic: Dutch (1–979); Flemish (1001–1184); Friesian
        (1401–1558); German (3001–5999)

PG   Slavic. Baltic, Albanian languages and literatures
Slavic (1–7925)
     Church Slavic (615–716); Bulgarian. Macedonian (801–
        1164); Serbo-Croatian (1201–1696); Slovenian
        (1801–1962); Russian. White Russian. Ukrainian
        (2001–3987); Czech. Slovak (4001–5546); Polish.
        Sorbian (5631–7446)
Baltic (8001–9146): Lithuanian (8501–8772); Latvian (8801–
     9146)
Albanian (9501–9678)

PH   Finno-Ugrian, Basque languages and literatures
Finnish (101–1109)
     Finnish (Proper) (101–405); Estonian (601–671); Lappish
        (701–735)
Ugrian. Hungarian (1201–3445)
Basque (5001–5490)

Oriental languages and literature

PJ General works (1–995)
Egyptian. Coptic (1001–2199)
Hamitic (2301–2551)
   Libyan group (2353–2367); Berber (2369–2399); Cushitic
      (2401–2539)
Semitic (3001–9293)
   Assyrian. Sumerian (3101–4083); Hebrew (4501–5192); Ara-
      maic (5201–5329); Syriac (5403–5809); Arabic (6001–
      8517); Ethiopian (9001–9293)

PK Indo-Iranian (1–6996)—including Vedic, Sanskrit, Pali, Assam-
      ese, Bengali, Hindi, Urdu, Hindustani, Sinhalese, Persian
Armenian (8001–8958)
Caucasian. Georgian (9001–9201)

PL Languages and literatures of Eastern Asia, Africa, Oceania
Japanese language and literature (501–889)
Korean language and literature (901–998)
Chinese language and literature (1001–3207)
Oceanic languages and literatures (5001–7511)
African languages and literatures (8000–8844)

PM
American Indian languages (101–7356)
Artificial languages (8001–9021)

Literature

PN Literary history and collections (General)
Criticism (80–99)
Authorship (101–249)
Literary history (441–1009)—including folk literature, fables,
      prose romances
Poetry (1010–1551)
The performing arts. Show business (1560–1590)
The drama (1600–3299)
   Dramatic composition (1660–1692)
   Special types of drama (1865–1999)—including tragedy,
      comedy, vaudeville, puppet plays, pantomimes, bal-
      let, radio and television broadcasts, motion pictures
   Dramatic representation. The theater (2000–3299)
Prose. Prose fiction (3311–3503)
Oratory. Elocution, recitations, etc. (4001–4355)

Letters (4400)
Essays (4500)
Journalism. The periodical press, etc. (4699–5650)
Collections of general literature (6011–6525)
  Quotations (6080–6095)
  Poetry (6099–6110)
  Drama (6110.5–6120)
  Orations (6121–6129)
  Letters (6130–6140)
  Essays (6141–6145)
  Wit and humor. Satire (6147–6231)
  Miscellaneous (6249–6525)—including anecdotes, aphorisms, maxims, mottoes, toasts, riddles, proverbs

PQ Romance literatures

PR English literature

PS American literature

PT Germanic literatures

PZ Fiction and juvenile literature

Q. SCIENCE (A few sections useful to the history student)

Q Science (General)
    *History

QA Mathematics
    Mathematical logic (8–10); Computer science, etc. (76); Elementary mathematics. Arithmetic (101–145); Algebra (152–299); Analysis (300–433); Geometry (443–699); Analytic mechanics (801–935)

QB Astronomy
    Practical and spherical astronomy (145–237); Geodesy (275–343); Theoretical astronomy and celestial mechanics (351–421); Astrophysics and descriptive astronomy (460–991)

QC Physics
    Weights and measures (81–119); Descriptive and experimental mechanics (120–168); Constitution and properties of matter. Atomic physics (171–197); Sound. Acoustics (220–246); Heat (251–338); Light. Optics (350–495);

Electricity and magnetism (501–768); Nuclear and particle physics. Atomic energy. Radioactivity (770–798); Geophysics. Cosmic physics (801–809); Geomagnetism (811–849); Meteorology (851–999)

QD Chemistry

QE Geology

QH Natural history
Nature conservation. Landscape protection (75–77); Microscopy (201–278); General biology (301–559)—including life, genetics, evolution, reproduction, ecology; Cytology (573–671)

QK Botany

QL Zoology

QM Human anatomy—including Human embryology (601–699)

QP Physiology

QR Microbiology

R. MEDICINE (A few sections useful to the history student)

R Medicine (General)
*History of medicine (131–684)
Medical education (735–847)
Medical physics. Electronics. Radiology, etc. (895)

RA Public aspects of medicine
Medicine and the state (5–418)
Public health. Hygiene. Preventive medicine (421–790)—including sanitation, disposal of the dead, transmission of disease, epidemics, quarantine, personal hygiene
Medical geography. Medical climatology and meteorology (791–954)
Medical centers. Hospitals. Clinics (960–998)

RB Pathology

RC Internal medicine

RD Surgery—including Wounds and injuries (92–96); Orthopedics (701–796)

RE Ophthalmology

RF Otorhinolaryngology

RG Gynecology and obstetrics

RJ Pediatrics

RK Dentistry

RL Dermatology

RM Therapeutics. Pharmacology

RS Pharmacy and materia medica

RT Nursing

RV Botanic, Thomsonian, and eclectic medicine

RX Homeopathy

RZ Other systems of medicine
   Chiropractic (201–265); Osteopathy (301–397); Mental healing
      (400–408)

S. AGRICULTURE (A few sections useful to the history student)

S Agriculture (General)
   Farm management. Farm economics (560–575); Agricultural
      chemistry and physics (583–589); Soils (590–599);
      Reclamation and irrigation of farm land (605–621);
      Soil conservation (622–627); Fertilizers and soil im-
      provement (631–669); Farm machinery and engineer-
      ing (671–760); Conservation of natural resources
      (900–972)—including Land conservation (950–954),
      Wildlife conservation (960–964), Recreational re-
      sources conservation (970–972)

SB Plant culture

SD Forestry
   Description of forest trees (383–385); Sylviculture (391–409);
      Conservation and protection (411–425); Forest res-
      erves (426–428); Exploitation and utilization (430–
      557)—including timber trees, logging, transportation,
      valuation; Forest policy and administration (561–668)

SF Animal culture

SH Fish culture and fisheries—including Angling (401–691)

SK Hunting
   Wildlife management. Game protection (351–579)

Camping. Outdoor life (601–608)

T. TECHNOLOGY (A few sections useful to the history student)

T Technology (General)

General engineering and civil engineering group

TA Engineering (General). Civil engineering (General)

TC Hydraulic engineering—including harbors and coast protective works, water-supply engineering, dams, canals, irrigation projects

TD Environmental technology. Sanitary engineering

TE Highway engineering. Roads and pavements

TF Railroad engineering and operation—including street railways

TG Bridge engineering

TH Building construction

Mechanical group

TJ Mechanical engineering and machinery

TK Electrical engineering. Electronics. Nuclear engineering

TL Motor vehicles. Aeronautics. Astronautics
Motor vehicles (1–390); Aeronautics (500–777); Rockets (780–785); Astronautics (787–4050)

Chemical group

TN Mining engineering. Metallurgy—including the mineral industries

TP Chemical technology

TR Photography

Composite group

TS Manufactures
Production management (155–193)—including quality control, production control, inventory control, product engineering; Packaging (195–198); Metal manufactures. Metalworking (200–770)—including forging, casting, stamping, instrument making, firearms, clocks, jew-

elry; Wood technology (800–937)—including lumber, furniture, chemical processing of wood; Leather industries. Tanning (940–1067); Paper manufacture. Wood-pulp industry (1080–1268); Textile industries (1300–1865); Rubber industry (1870–1935); Animal products (1950–1981); Cereals and flour. Milling industry (2120–2159); Tobacco industry (2220–2283)

TT Handicrafts. Arts and crafts

Manual training (161–169); Woodworking. Furniture making, etc. (180–200); Metalworking (205–267); Painting. Industrial painting (300–382); Clothing manufacture. Dressmaking. Tailoring (490–695); Needlework. Decorative crafts (697–910)

TX Home economics

U. MILITARY SCIENCE—For military history, *see* D–F (A few sections useful to the history student)

U Military science (General)

Military life, manners and customs (750–773)

History of arms and armor (800–897)

UA Armies: Organization, description, facilities, etc.—including the military situation, policy, defenses of individual countries

UB Military administration

UC Maintenance and transportation

UD Infantry

UE Cavalry. Armored and mechanized cavalry

UF Artillery

UG Military engineering—including fortification, chemical warfare, signaling, air warfare

UH Other services—including medical and sanitary service, public relations, social welfare services, recreation

V. NAVAL SCIENCE—For naval history, *see* D–F (A few sections useful to the history student)

V Naval science (General)

Naval life, manners and customs (720–743)

War vessels: Construction, armament, etc. (750–980)
Fleet ballistic missile systems (990–995)

VA Navies: Organization, description, facilities, etc.—including the naval situation and policy of individual countries

VB Naval administration

VC Naval maintenance

VD Naval seamen

VE Marines

VF Naval ordnance

VG Minor services of navies—including communications, bands, air service, medical service, public relations, social work, etc.

VK Navigation. Merchant marine
Marine hydography. Hydrographic surveying (588–597)
Tide and current tables (600–794)
Pilot guides. Sailing directions (798–997)
Lighthouse service (1000–1249)
Shipwrecks and fires (1250–1299)
Saving of life and property (1300–1491)
Pilots and pilotage (1500–1661)

VM Naval architecture. Shipbuilding
Marine engineering (600–965)
Submarine diving (975–989)

Z. BIBLIOGRAPHY AND LIBRARY SCIENCE (A few sections useful to the history student)
Books in general
History of books and bookmaking (4–8)
Writing (40–115)
Autographs. Signatures (40–42); Calligraphy, Penmanship (43–45); Copying processes (48); Typewriting (49–51); Shorthand (53–102); Cryptography (103–104); Paleography (105–115)
Book industries and trade
Printing (116–265); Bookbinding (266–276); Bookselling and publishing (278–549)
Libraries and library science (662–1000)
Architecture and planning of the library (679–680)

The collection. The books (687–717)—including acquisition, cataloging, classification, etc.

Libraries (719–876)—including histories, reports, etc.

Library catalogs and bulletins (881–980)

Private libraries. Book collecting (987–997)

Booksellers' catalogs. Book prices (998–1000)

Bibliography (1001–8999)

Anonyms and pseudonyms (1041–1107); National bibliography (1201–4980); Subject bibliography (5051–7999); Personal bibliography (8001–8999)

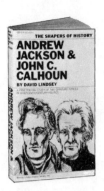

With information on Indian nationalism, the political scene in Gandhi's time, his own religious evolution, his ethics and economics, and his attitudes toward war and untouchability. $2.95

A serious attempt to deal with Jimmy Carter and what he stands for, with emphasis on his past record as state senator and Governor of Georgia, his campaign for the presidency and a look at his administration. $2.95

The dual biographies in the series present a contrastive view. They offer fresh, previously unexplored perspectives and reveal surprising similarities and differences. $3.95

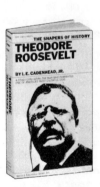

Jefferson & Hamilton presents history as it was lived by two young men. The problems they faced and the controversies that divided them are presented through a balanced treatment. $4.95

Thomas Wendel presents the reader with the varied — sometimes conflicting aspects of Franklin's life as a printer, inventor, politician, land speculator, statesman, and philosopher. $3.50

Cowboy, hunter, soldier, author, politician: our 26th President held the attention and enthusiasm of the nation perhaps as no other President has since. I. E. Cadenhead, Jr., presents an objective but vivid account of Roosevelt's controversial career. $3.95

Barron's Essentials/
The Efficient Study Guides

Handbooks that describe various political systems, and ideologies. Each offers analytical surveys, study guides, references, and review material.

American Government, Essentials of 688 pp., $5.50

American History, Vol. I To 1877 480 pp., $5.50

American History, Vol. 2 Since 1865 508 pp., $5.50

Communism, Classic and Contemporary 320 pp., $3.50

Comparative Government, Essentials of 224 pp., $2.95

Democracy, Essentials of 336 pp., $3.95

Economics, Its Nature and Importance 512 pp., $6.50

Geography, Principles of (Physical & Cultural) 336 pp., $4.50

Physical Geography, Principles of 224 pp., $4.50

Political Parties, Essentials of 224 pp., $2.50

Political Science, Essentials of 336 pp., $2.95

Socialism 256 pp., $3.50

World History 480 pp., $3.50

How to Prepare for the Advanced Placement Examinations in American History

William O. Kellogg 320 pp., $5.50 Complete course guide for advanced placement and academic enrichment classes. Contains 8 review units with essay and multiple-choice questions; work in essay preparation, vocabulary-building, current affairs, anthologies of key documents and readings; and a model AP test.

The Meaning of the Constitution

Angela Roddey Holder 128 pp., $2.95 A complete analysis of the major American document—how it relates to current issues and court decisions. Includes explanations of amendments, the most recent amendments, and current issues such as wiretapping and privacy. A non-technical approach to law.

The Black Almanac

From Involuntary Servitude (1619—1860) to the Age of Disillusionment (1964—1976)
Alton Hornsby, Jr. 304 pp., $5.95 A chronicle of the historical events affecting black Americans since their arrival in the United States. It includes biographical details, institutions, events, court decisions, laws, and documents affecting the black American.

All prices subject to change without notice.
At your local bookseller or order direct adding 10% postage plus applicable sales tax.
Barron's Educational Series, Inc., 113 Crossways Park Drive, Woodbury, N.Y.

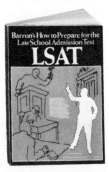
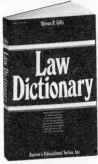